Practical Kitten Care

James DeBitetto, D.V.M.

Practical Kitten Care

James DeBitetto, D.V.M.

Howell Book House
A Simon & Schuster Macmillan Company
1633 Broadway
New York, NY 10019-6785

Book design by Douglas & Gayle, Ltd.

Library of Congress Cataloging-in-Publication Data
DeBitetto, James.
    Practical kitten care: an easy-to-understand manual for the
    health and care of your kitten / by James Debitetto.
        p. cm.
    Includes index.
    ISBN 0-87605-763-6
    1. Kittens. 2.Kittens—Health. I. Title.
SF447.D39   96-24293
636.8'083—dc20   CIP
    4 5 6 7 8 9 10   97 98 99 00 01

Contents

Acknowledgements

Because this is my third book with Howell Book House, it is important for me to thank the publisher, Sean Frawley, and my editor, Dominique DeVito. They have been inspirational and so supportive—I could not have asked for a better team and publisher. Thanks again so much.

My staff has now put up with me for three books and all I can say is "Thanks again, guys." A deep and heartfelt thanks to Katie Baldwin, Penny Kohlman, and Jacqueline Rieg. They are the best staff a veterinarian could ever ask for. They were also very generous in allowing me to photograph their kittens for parts of the book. A very special thanks to staff member Pam Koerner, who helped me with the grooming section and most of the instructional photographs. Her champion Maine Coon, Tiffany, was a perfect model.

A thanks to Dr. Marjorie Neaderland, my dear friend and colleague, for supplying photographs of cat eyes and her continued expertise as a veterinary ophthalmologist. Thanks to Ray Crawford for his help in medical photography, and Tammy Thomas from Pet Pics for use of one of her professional shoots.

I would like to extend a sincere thanks to a dear friend of mine who really taught me how to be a cat fancier, Pat Bender. She is the founder of Rags R Us Ragdolls, and knows more about cats than I could ever hope to. Thank you so much, Pat.

Lastly, I would like to thank my family: my parents, Dr. and Mrs. Dominick DeBitetto, for a lifetime of caring and love, and my brother, Bob, for his work on the contracts and years of legal and personal advice. Thank you to my in-laws, Mr. and Mrs. Frank Imschweiler, for all their love and support these last eighteen years. To my beautiful wife, Donna, who has been my soul mate and companion through it all—I love you more each day.

Introduction

Congratulations on your new kitten! There is nothing more endearing and enjoyable as a new kitten—fuzzy, cute, and playful. Many of us had kittens growing up, and if you didn't, you might want one now for your family or yourself. Kittens provide hours of fun and entertainment, not to mention endless love.

Many of my clients say that they would rather sit and watch their kitten at night than the television.

Cats are quickly surpassing dogs as the number one national pet, and those who have cats tend to have more than one. There are 2.1 cats per cat family, and almost 60 million cats nationwide. Let's face it, cats are certainly easier to care for than dogs. They require less space, time, training, and energy than dogs. The fact that you can litter-box train your kitten means that you don't have to take him out for walks like you do a dog. Many people keep their cats indoors. Also, most people keep their cats home when they go away and have someone come in every day to take care of them, eliminating the need for boarding kennels. For many busy, overworked people, cats are the ideal pet—easy to care for, fairly independent and forever giving in the love department. For children, kittens are the stuff dreams are made of.

The whole emphasis of this book is to make kitten care fun, practical, helpful and *simple*. This book is written for the novice kitten owner, but experienced cat fanciers will learn a lot, too. And unlike most of the big cat textbooks out there, you can pick it up and use it without going to veterinary school first. All of the most important and common topics are covered:

- Bringing a kitten home
- Concerns for pregnant women
- Kitten introductions into a household
- Vaccines and wormings
- Common viral diseases
- Health maintenance
- Feeding and nutrition
- Spaying and neutering
- First aid and household dangers
- Kittens at cat shows
- Kitten handling
- Encyclopedia of kitten pediatrics (part II)

Courtesy of Rags are Us, Pat Bender

I have included, throughout the book, a quick and easy reference graphic to alert you if the disease being described is contagious to other cats or people. This is good to know at-a-glance so you can start taking necessary precautions immediately.

If you see this graphic, it means that this particular disease is contagious to other cats.

If you see this graphic, it means that this particular disease is contagious to people.

Have fun, learn a lot, and most of all, bond with your new kitten. Your reward will be a lifetime of purrs, bonks, and love. As with all self-help books, use this as a guide and consult your veterinarian regarding specific questions about your kitten.

Chapter 1

Finding and Providing For Your New Kitten

The first thing you need to do is find a kitten; a healthy, happy, socialized kitten. By "kitten," I mean a young cat, certainly under six months of age, and often under three months. Finding a kitten might sound easy, but you need to keep certain things in mind, depending on where you go looking. I describe the people and places who offer kittens in the following sections. If you already have a kitten, reading the section that applies to you anyway could still give you some helpful tips.

Cat Breeders

Many people buy pedigree kittens from cat breeders. A *breeder* is a person who professionally breeds cats to sell and/or show. Suppose you wanted to

This kitten is almost old enough to leave Mom—but not yet!

1

purchase a Persian kitten. You could find a Persian cat breeder in your area, or a breeder who ships kittens to anywhere in the country. Ideally, you get a breeder's name from someone else who bought a kitten from them. If not, however, you can look in your local newspaper under the pet section. Cat magazines have listings in the back, or you can call national organizations for listings of registered breeders (see Appendix I for helpful addresses and phone numbers). Your local veterinarian also can assist you.

Breeders usually have a range of ages of kittens for sale, from six weeks to six months old. Kittens under three months of age are the most popular. You can expect to pay several hundred dollars for a quality pedigree kitten.

You want to make sure the breeder is registered with a national cat registry and has been breeding cats for at least five years (long enough to be sure their cats are free of genetic defects). They should be able to give you a certificate of pedigree with the kitten to prove it's a pure breed. Find out whether they offer a written guarantee for the kitten's health, and make sure they'll give you a refund or exchange if the kitten develops a disease or genetic problem within the first year. Reputable breeders are more than happy to meet these conditions. If they're reluctant, or refuse, you don't want to do business with them—find another breeder.

Pet Stores

Many pet stores sell pedigree and non-pedigree kittens. Most of them are young—under 12 weeks of age. They are often kept together in a pen or crate, which is great for display purposes, but not so great if one of the kittens is ill, because then all the kittens get exposed. The kittens are often placed in the main area of the store so people can get close and even hold them if they want. Although this is a bit risky (kids tend to drop kittens when they squirm), it does socialize them early, which is a good thing.

If you're interested in a pet store kitten, try to find out how the store got the animals—from a breeder, pet wholesaler, or maybe just a neighborhood family looking to place a litter of their cat. This matters, because it should reflect the price of the kitten. Prices at pet stores can range from "free to a good home," to a minimal fee of about $25, to several hundred dollars for a pedigree kitten.

Like breeders, most pet stores give a written guarantee for the health and pedigree of the kitten. These guarantees usually are good until the kitten is 6–12 months old. They are also willing to exchange or replace a sick kitten. In some states, pet stores must offer to pay for veterinary care up to the purchase price of the kitten in the event that the owner doesn't want a replacement or refund, which does come into play because many people quickly become attached to their new kitten.

Animal Shelters

I commend you if you choose or have chosen to get your kitten at an animal shelter! Every adoption helps, with so many homeless animals in this country. Animal shelters often have a wide variety of ages and breeds; as you can imagine, the young healthy kittens go fast. You might have to go on a waiting list for one. Most shelters have many older kittens that need homes. You might want to consider one of these.

The problem with adopting a kitten from a shelter is that you basically have to take what you can get. Shelters rarely have the resources for extensive health maintenance on their rescued animals, so the kitten you adopt probably won't have vaccines, might not have been examined by a veterinarian, and could have worms and fleas or other health problems. It's up to you to make sure a veterinarian examines your kitten. The cost of these procedures should be offset by the minimal fee you pay at the shelter and the satisfaction of knowing you adopted a needy kitten. Many veterinarians give discounts to people who adopt shelter animals. Some shelters also have a return policy if things don't work out, but rarely do they guarantee health.

Feline Rescue Organizations

These organizations usually are nonprofit groups of volunteers who spend their time rescuing and saving orphaned kittens and cats. I personally work with such a group and find the work they do fabulous. The volunteers take homeless, orphaned, or abandoned cats and put them into foster homes for adoption. Before they can be adopted, the cats and kittens are vaccinated, wormed, and examined by a veterinarian, as well as tested for the Feline Leukemia and Feline Aids viruses. Lastly, all cats are spayed (females) or neutered (males).

You might pay a bit more for one of these kittens (up to $50), but you're getting a healthy, vaccinated, tested, and "fixed" kitten. The Cat Fanciers' Association (CFA) can put you in touch with rescue organizations—or ask your vet.

Regardless of where you get it, here are some tips on finding a healthy kitten:

Before You Get Your Kitten

There are other considerations before you get a kitten. The first and most important is: Who is the kitten for? Is it for a three-year-old child, or a spouse? Where will the kitten live? Whose job is it to feed it and change the litter box? If you're a parent and you're getting a kitten for your child, don't think that you're off the hook. As the adult, you will be responsible for the care and well-being of the kitten. Sit down and have a talk with your family.

Tips for Finding a Healthy Kitten

- Find a kitten who is active, playful and bright-eyed—sick kittens are quiet, sluggish and thin.
- Stay clear of kittens who constantly sneeze, cough, vomit, or have diarrhea.
- Check for runny eyes or nose, or heavy breathing, which can indicate respiratory disease.
- Look for signs of a bloated abdomen, which can indicate internal parasites (nearly 80 percent of kittens are born with worms).
- Look for fecal staining at the rectum, which can suggest diarrhea or colitis.
- Pick a kitten who has a hardy appetite, not one who requires force-feeding.
- Pick a kitten who has experienced plenty of handling—such kittens generally are better socialized and, consequently, make better pets.
- Have a veterinarian examine your new kitten soon after you get him. Your vet can identify problems early, which can lead to early diagnosis and treatment.

If you have children, you'll need to have a family discussion that covers the following angles:

- Establishing the kitten's sleeping accommodations
- Feeding the kitten
- Cleaning the litter box
- Holding the kitten gently
- Understanding the concept of general respect for living things
- Ensuring care for the kitten when no one is home

Kitten-Proofing Your Home

The very first thing to do after you pick out your new kitten is to make your home a safe place for the kitten to live. To do that, you need to remove all things a kitten could get into that could be dangerous. The first rule of preparing a home: Kittens get into everything: closets, drawers, cabinets, potted plants, garbage cans, Christmas trees, toilet bowls, refrigerators, drapery, sofa cushions, garages, and much more. I know I'm making them sound like little Terminators, but it's true. Kittens get into places you've never given a second (or first) thought.

You must take precautions to remove all unsafe things from their reach. If you have children, this becomes more difficult. Pick up all toys under two inches in length. Also pick up paper clips, coins, rubber bands, ribbons, tape, yarn or string, and any other small object a kitten could try to swallow.

Close all cabinet doors, and keep all cleaners, chemicals, and toxic substances out of kitten's reach. If your house is undergoing construction, be very careful of paints, paint thinner, adhesives, insulation, lead paint, asbestos, nails, and other supplies. Excessive dust and fumes during construction also can harm your kitten.

Be careful of electric cords, like those coming out of a lamp or appliance. Kittens can chew on these cords and get electrocuted. Keep them up off the floor and out of the kitten's reach. Another thing to keep away from kittens is household plants. Many are toxic, fresh or dried (see Chapter 5 for a list of poisonous plants).

Kittens are naturally curious and tend to seek high places. You might find your kitten on top of cabinets, refrigerators, wood piles, rafters, or curtain rods. Because it's nearly impossible to keep them away from these spots, make sure your windows are screened or closed. It's common for cats and kittens to fall out of unscreened windows in urban apartments. In fact, the injuries that occur from such falls are called "High Rise Syndrome."

Pick a spot for the food and water bowls. Most people use the kitchen floor. Notice I said food *and* water. Some people erroneously think kittens don't need water. All animals need water—fresh, clean water, changed several times daily. Keep the water bowl within two feet of the food dish, so your kitten will learn that where there's food, there's also water. Don't be surprised if your kitten prefers your faucet for his water. Most cats instinctively know that cold, running water is cleaner than warm, stagnant water. I know many people who keep their faucets trickling cold water just so their cat can jump up on the sink and drink. If this isn't feasible for you, just change the water in the bowl frequently and add an ice cube or two on hot days.

Litter Box Etiquette

Pick a place for the litter box away from the food bowls. Most people use the laundry room, basement, or bathroom for the litter box. Remember that cats are very particular about where they go to the bathroom, and they don't like to use a litter box that's near anything noisy or disruptive. So don't put it right next to the washer or dryer, for example, or by the furnace or beneath a frequently used staircase. Select a quiet spot where your kitten can go in peace.

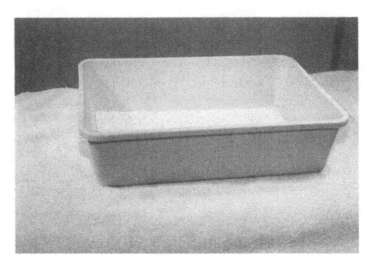

A typical litter box.

Litter boxes come in several types: flat trays, deep dish, covered, and potty seats for the toilet. I have found the best is the uncovered tray, at least two inches deep. Your kitten can easily hop into such a box, and he kicks minimal litter out on the floor (you'll quickly learn that kittens like to scratch and dig in the litter, often spilling it out of the box).

There are three basic types of litter on the market:

- **Clay.** Some clay litter comes with deodorizers, while some doesn't; some clay litter brands are dust free

- **Clumping.** Clumping litters are so named because they clump with moisture so that you can scoop out the soiled litter but leave the rest

- **Paper pellets.** Paper pellets often consist of recycled newspaper made into absorbent pellets

Basically, all the litter has to do is be able to absorb moisture from the urine and stool and give the kitten something to scratch in. Additional properties that litter can feature include deodorizers, fresh scents, dust free formulas, and environmentally friendly litter.

Don't use litters heavy in deodorants—some cats are allergic to them. The same goes for dusty litter. It makes many kittens sneeze.

Whatever type of litter you use, *keep the litter box clean.* That means that if you use a clay or paper litter, change the entire box daily. Use a disinfectant to wash the box out, then dry it, and refill it with about one to two inches of fresh litter. Don't let stool or soiled litter sit in the box—it can increase your kitten's likelihood of getting an infection. If you use the clumping litter, scoop out the soiled clumps daily, then change the litter and wash the box weekly.

If you have more than one cat in your household, you might need two litter boxes. Some cats are so fastidious that they won't use a box if another cat (especially a new kitten) has soiled it. Many of my clients have told me, "Once I got the new kitten, my other cat wouldn't use the box and is going on the floor next to it!"

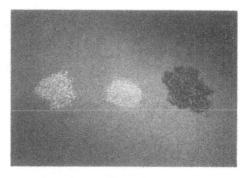

Three different litters (l-r): clay, clumping, compressed newspaper.

Toys and Other Stuff

Loads of kitten and cat toys are available, ranging from furry mice to catnip-coated scratching posts, from dangling toys for doorknobs to plastic donuts with balls to chase inside. You can find carpeted kitty condos with one, two, or three perches—some people get window perch seats so their kitten can watch the birds outside. You can get fake mice on a string and feathers on a wand. And that's all for the cat, not to mention all the different merchandise for you, like T-shirts, mugs, earrings, key chains, cat carriers, and art work, all in honor of our feline friends. You see all this stuff at pet stores, in pet catalogs, and at cat shows, to name a few common places.

What's necessary and what's not? One *must* is a scratching post, which is just a wooden post covered in carpet, that the kitten uses to sharpen and maintain his nails (more on this in Chapter 2, under "Declawing"). I'm sure you'd rather he use a scratching post than the furniture.

A kitten involved in a favorite activity: playing! *Pam Koerner*

Because cats are natural climbers, your kitten might
like an indoor "cat tree." *Pam Koerner*

Because kittens love *and need* to play, you can experiment with the
various toys to see what your kitten likes best. You also can make toys from
things like old paper towel rolls and toilet paper rolls, knotted socks, and so
on. Although kittens love to play with string, they can get in *big* trouble if
they swallow it, so keep those balls of yarn tightly wrapped or out of sight.

Your Kitten and Your Family

Introducing your new kitten into your household can be a delicate matter,
especially if you have children or other pets. It's simple if it's just you and/or
other adults, but when you factor in kids and pets, things can become a bit
tricky.

Kittens with Children

The parents are the ones who should handle introducing a young kitten to
children. Families often come to my office with a brand new kitten and young
children. I take time to go over tips on how to bring the children and kitten
together, and I spend more time with families who have children younger
than seven. The following are some guidelines for parents:

- **Go slow.**   The first thing most kids want to do is hold the kitten. *It is
  natural to nurture.* The problem is that knowing how to hold the kitten
  gently, without squeezing or dropping it, doesn't seem to come naturally.
  Kittens are fragile, and you need to show children how to be careful not
  to harm them when they hold them.

- **Teach respect.**   Parents should teach their children to respect living things. This means doing what is right for the animal, and not always what the child might want.

- **Let each child get introduced.**   Let each child hold the kitten in turn and for a specified time, like a minute or so. Then put the kitten down or in its bed. Don't overwhelm him all at once. Kittens get scared very easily.

- **Get the kids involved.**   Have the kids help feed, clean, and care for the kitten. This involvement forms a bond between the child and the kitten that will last for a lifetime.

- **Don't rush.**   Expect it to take several weeks before your kitten feels comfortable in his new home. Give him space and love. Don't be surprised if he spends the first few days hiding under the bed. As endearing as the pitter-patter of little Junior's feet is to us, it can seem about as wonderful as an earthquake to a kitten.

Kittens with Other Pets

Bringing a kitten home to a household in which other pets already are entrenched can prove tricky. Animals naturally establish a hierarchy, or order, among themselves. This social structure is a delicate balance that can take months to achieve, whether it's dogs with dogs, cats with cats, or dogs with cats. Dogs quickly establish an alpha figure who is the "top dog" and to whom all other dogs are subordinate. Cats also are very territorial and establish boundaries, order, protocol, and ceremony. When you bring a new member into the household, it can throw a big wrench in the works.

Each pet already has an idea of how things work in the house, and where they fit in the scheme of things. Your new kitten will have to feel his own way, learn the ropes, and find a way to belong. You can take some of the following steps to help ease the process:

1. Bring something of the new kitten's into the house before you actually bring him home, so the other pets can get used to the new kitten's smell, as well as the idea of having him around.

2. When you bring your kitten home for the first time, keep him in his cat carrier while you let the other pets explore him. They will probably sniff, stare, and maybe bark or hiss. That's okay. That's their way of saying "You're low man on the totem pole." If things get a bit tense, take the carrier away to another room. Let things cool off a bit, then try again. Keep the kitten in a separate room during this process. He should have his own food and water dish, and litter box. You might notice your other pets sniffing under the door, or talking to the kitten through it. If so, that's great; they're getting acquainted.

Cats and dogs, like this kitten and Bichon Frise,
can often make great friends. *Katie Baldwin*

3. After a day or so of this carrier peek-a-boo and through-the-door
communication, you're ready to try putting them together. *Do not* just
leave them alone. You must stay and supervise the event. If things get
uneasy, take the kitten back to his room and try again tomorrow.
Even if things seem to go well, return the kitten to his room when
you're too busy to chaperone.

4. After a few days of supervised playtimes, you can try putting them
together in the same room, but don't leave them alone. If a problem
crops up, you'll hear it. Only after you are convinced that all animals are
getting along satisfactorily should you leave them alone for longer
periods. This whole adjustment period can last a month, or even a little
longer, so hang in there. It's worth the effort to have everyone get along.

Inside or Outside Cat?

This is an age-old question: "Should I let my kitten go outside, or keep
him in?" Many people are torn over this decision. They think that cats need
to go outside, and if they don't let them, they're wrought with guilt. Or, they
let their kitten go outside, and then spend the next hour nervously watching
out the window hoping all is well. I have seen both—cats who go outside
every day of their lives for fifteen years without a mishap, and the case where
Shadow escapes once and gets hit by a car.

So what are you to do? Realize that if you do send your kitten outside, you
are exposing him to dangers like cars, neighborhood bully cats, roaming dogs,
mean kids, wild animals, and trees from which to fall out. I tell my clients

their kittens will be much safer inside, but if you insist on letting your kitty out, here are guidelines to follow:

Guidelines for Outdoor Kittens and Cats

- Never let your kitten out alone until six months of age and until he's had all his vaccines.
- Let your kitten out only during the day, never at night, when wild animals, stray pets, and cars pose the greatest threat.
- Go outside with your kitten for the first five or so times to teach him the boundaries of the yard. Chase him back into the yard when he strays so he learns where not to go.
- Never let your kitten outside if you live near a busy road.
- Keep your kitten up-to-date on all inoculations before you let him outside, in case he encounters another diseased animal.
- Call your kitten inside for his evening feeding. Then keep him in even if he drives you crazy! Nighttime is when most mishaps occur.
- Have your kitten spayed or neutered before letting him outside, to avoid contributing to the overpopulation problem.

Chapter 2

First Visit to the Veterinarian

How are things going so far? I'm sure you're now enjoying your kitten. Chapter 1 focused primarily on providing fundamental kitten care advice—things you need to know right away. This chapter begins to get more technical. Don't worry, I'll keep things simple. However, it is time to take your new kitten in for his first veterinary visit. The veterinarian performs several standard procedures for young kittens, including vaccines, worming, blood tests for infectious diseases, and a physical exam for birth defects. I'm going to cover each one, beginning with the most important and first thing your kitten needs—his *vaccines*.

Bring your kitten to the veterinarian as soon as you get him.

Vaccines

What is a vaccine? That's a good question. A *vaccine* is a biological suspension that, when given to an animal, imparts immunity against a specific infectious disease. In plain English, a vaccine immunizes, or protects, the animal against a given disease.

When your veterinarian injects a vaccine, your kitten becomes *immunized* against a disease, meaning his immune system starts to make proteins, called *antibodies*, which circulate in the bloodstream and bind to the disease causing organism, rendering it powerless to cause disease. These antibodies can last anywhere from one to three years, depending on which rabies vaccine the veterinarian uses.

There are different types of vaccines, and different ways they can be administered. The two most common types of vaccines are killed and attenuated:

- **Killed.** Killed vaccines are a suspension of particles of the virus. The organisms are dead, so they can't cause disease. These vaccines usually are mild and don't last as long as other types.

- **Attenuated.** (*also called* **Modified Live**) Attenuated vaccines are made of live viruses that have been changed or altered in some way so that they cannot cause disease. These are stronger than killed vaccines and usually last longer.

A kitten receives a vaccine in one of three different ways:

- **Subcutaneous injection.** An injection given under the skin of the scruff, or neck.

- **Intramuscular injection.** An injection given in the muscle of the lower back or leg.

- **Intranasal.** Nose drops in the nostrils.

Your veterinarian knows the best ways in which to administer the various vaccines.

Diseases Against Which Kittens Are Vaccinated

Several common vaccines are routinely given to kittens. Starting at six weeks of age, kittens get the first of a series of vaccines, called the *distemper* vaccine, which is abbreviated, FVRCP-C. This series of vaccines (boostered annually) actually attacks a combination of four different viruses.

Three other vaccines are available to immunize kittens against other potentially harmful or fatal diseases: rabies, feline leukemia virus, and feline infectious peritonitis.

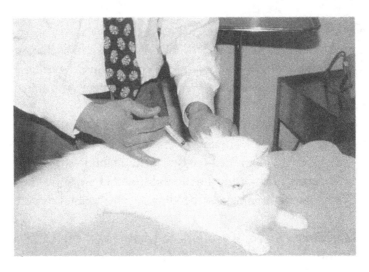

This kitten is being given a vaccine subcutaneously. *Pam Koerner*

The following eight sections look closely at each of the four different viral diseases against which the distemper (FVRCP-C) vaccine is designed to protect, and then at each of the other three in turn (including an extra section on the feline immunodeficiency virus, because it often accompanies the feline leukemia virus, even though no vaccine currently is available for it.)

Your veterinarian can tell you which vaccines your kitten needs based on where you live and whether your kitten goes outside.

FVR (Feline Rhinotracheitis)

FVR is an upper respiratory virus that mainly affects kittens. It is a *herpes* virus. Don't worry, people can't get this one. This virus infects the upper respiratory passages of cats. The virus enters the kitten's respiratory passages when it inhales air in which the virus is floating. Symptoms occur within five days. The common scenario is a young kitten—usually under 12 weeks old—who has crusted, closed eyes, mild fever, sneezing, coughing, nasal and eye discharge with loss of appetite and dehydration. You also can find blisters in the mouth and on the tongue. Some of these kittens get a secondary bronchitis or pneumonia. These kittens need quick and steady support with antibiotics, fluids, and nutritional/vitamin supplements. The prognosis is fair to guarded, depending on the severity of the respective case. These kittens remain infective for up to 14 days and should be kept away from other cats during that time.

Feline Calicivirus

This is another upper respiratory virus of kittens and young cats. The virus is very similar to the rhinotracheitis seen in FVR. The symptoms, incubation period, treatment, and prognosis are similar. The major difference is that cali-civirus can cause more severe oral blisters and mouth ulcers, and often is asso-ciated with bronchitis and pneumonia.

Feline Panleukopenia

This virus greatly resembles the *parvovirus* of dogs (for those of you who own both cats and dogs). Again, young kittens are the most susceptible and they catch the virus through oral contami-nation with bodily fluids of an infected cat. Symptoms can occur quickly, within a day or so, and are high fever (above 103°F), brain damage with neurological problems, vomiting and mucus-yellow diarrhea, dehydra-tion, and a pronounced reduction of disease-fighting white blood cells (WBC). The intestines are bloated and can become nonfunctional. Treat-ment is geared to correct the dehydration and prevent secondary infections resulting from the low WBC count. Antibiotics, electrolyte fluids, and nutri-tional/vitamin supplements are given aggressively. Many of these kittens die within several days, making the prognosis poor. Those kittens who do survive have residual neurological problems from brain damage—specifically to the cerebellum (which deals with coordination and movement, among other less obvious activities).

In pregnant females who become infected, the feline panleukopenia virus causes a deformed and smaller than normal cerebellum (*cerebellar hypoplasia*) in developing fetuses. Affected kittens live a handicapped life, but are adorable in their own way. They are very shaky and unstable on their feet, so don't expect the normal feline grace. I've seen hundreds of these kittens over the last eleven years, and only one has been so severely afflicted that it sim-ply couldn't function—and that's the only one I've had to euthanize.

Chlamydia (Pneumonitis)

This isn't really a virus. *Chlamydia psittaci* is a bacteria, and causes chronic upper respiratory disease and conjunctivitis (inflammation of the eye). These infections often recur and can cause frequent relapses. Cases aren't often fatal, but they can cause a little kitten considerable misery with sneezing, swollen eyes, eye and nasal discharge, fever, and breathing distress. If a kitten experiences recurrent conjunctivitis, you should suspect chlamydia. This organism also infects many birds, so kittens living with a pet bird are more likely to be exposed. In fact, it can keep circulating back and forth between the bird and the kitten. Cases of pneumonitis are treated aggressively with systemic and ophthalmic antibiotics. The prognosis is fair, because this dis-ease causes more morbidity than mortality. There have been reported cases of people getting chlamydia.

Rabies

Rabies is a fatal viral disease that affects all warm-blooded animals. Many states now require rabies vaccination for all pets. Rabies spreads through the bite of an infected animal because the virus thrives in infected animals' saliva. Several wildlife species carry the virus, including bats, raccoons, skunks, foxes, and other predatory animals.

This virus enters the nervous system and travels until it reaches the brain. The incubation period ranges from weeks to months. Typical symptoms are behavioral and neurologic changes, including changes in voice, gait, aggression or friendliness; dilated pupils; paralyzed jaw with drooling (hence the well-known "foaming at the mouth" symptom); paralysis; seizures; and eventual death.

Of all pets, cats show the highest incidence of rabies, owing to their hunting instincts. The only way to diagnose rabies is to do an autopsy and take brain samples to test for the rabies virus. Rabies cannot be treated, and given the serious threat a rabid animal poses to people, the pet is always humanely destroyed. County health departments conduct post-exposure treatments for anyone who might have been exposed to the rabid animal. *Since this is such a serious potential human hazard, be sure to vaccinate your kitten for rabies as soon as he turns 12 weeks old.* There are one-, two- and three-year vaccines on the market, so ask your vet which one is best for your kitten. I use the three-year vaccine because it increases the chances of the cat population being current for rabies.

Feline Leukemia Virus (FeLV)

This is a highly infectious lethal virus that affects only cats. This complicated virus can cause a variety of ailments, ranging from immune suppression to cancer. A kitten can catch feline leukemia in one of two ways: being born from a leukemia positive mother or via physical contact with an infected cat or its bodily fluids (blood, saliva, feces, milk, or urine). *Recent studies have shown that as many as one-third of all outdoor cats carry the virus.* After a kitten is exposed to the virus, three outcomes are possible:

1. The kitten becomes symptomatic and dies within weeks.
2. The kitten experiences a mild case and becomes a "carrier" of the virus, meaning, it's always infected and can transmit the disease to other cats, but doesn't die from the disease itself.
3. The kitten experiences chronic bouts of illness on and off for months to years before finally dying of the disease.

The leukemia virus causes two distinct groups of illnesses: immune suppression-related diseases, and cancers of the blood, intestines, or lymphatic cells. Kittens who have the virus appear dull, have a fever, are dehydrated, have profound anemia (low blood count), and often have respiratory disease, like bronchitis or pneumonia. They usually eat little to nothing and are lethargic. As the disease progresses, the white blood cell counts drop, leaving the kitten open to any secondary infection and to cancer of any of the lymph nodes or blood. By this stage, the kitten becomes critically ill with vomiting, diarrhea, and extreme weight loss.

If the kitten does survive this initial stage of the disease, it becomes a carrier of the virus. The diagnosis is very simple with a blood test for the presence of the virus. Treatment mainly consists of supportive care with antibiotics, fluids, nutritional supplements, and sometimes chemotherapy if the kitten has cancer. Unfortunately, about half of the kittens die within six months of the onset, and up to 80 percent die within the first three years.

Fortunately, excellent vaccines are available for protection against feline leukemia. Most kittens are tested by 12 weeks of age, and if negative, given the first of two leukemia vaccines. This vaccine is especially important for outdoor cats and kittens brought into a multi-cat household, because they have a higher risk of exposure. I recommend the vaccine even for indoor cats who might have exposure to an outdoor cat through a screened window or door, because cats can spit or spray urine at each other through the screen. A second vaccine is given three weeks later and an annual booster is required. The vaccine is greater than 95-percent effective and a great tool in the fight against this lethal feline virus.

I have had dozens of FeLV-positive patients recover from their initial illness and do fine. Because they're more susceptible to disease, you need to take extra precautions to maintain good health, such as good nutrition and low environmental stress.

Feline Immunodeficiency Virus (FIV)

FIV is the latest virus to hit the feline world. It's related to the feline leukemia virus described in the preceding section, and to the human AIDS virus. Don't panic—*people with AIDS cannot give their virus to their cat, and cats with FIV cannot give it to people.* FIV and AIDS do, however, share many similarities. The virus causes a profound immunosuppression and low white blood cell count. It doesn't cause cancer the way the leukemia virus sometimes does. Even though no vaccine is available for FIV, I include this discussion of it here because of its close link to the feline leukemia virus.

The good news is that this virus is not as contagious nor as prevalent as the leukemia virus. FIV occurs in only approximately three percent of the domestic cat population. Like AIDS, FIV spreads venereally or through blood products, which means your kitten can get infected by breeding with or being bitten by an infected cat. If your kitten is neutered, you don't have to worry about the breeding. But, if he goes outside and fights with the neighborhood stray, he stands a good chance of becoming infected. Recent studies have shown that up to fifty percent of cats with feline leukemia also have FIV.

The FIV virus causes a profound anemia and immunosuppression. White blood cells drop, leaving the kitten susceptible to all kinds of secondary infections. Most of these kittens have pneumonia, fevers over 103°F, breathing distress, pale mucus membranes, poor coats, and are thin and dehydrated. Most of them have no appetite and can have vomiting and diarrhea, which can be bloody. All the external lymph nodes (or glands) are enlarged.

Although rare, a small percentage of kittens survive this initial virus stage with vigorous support of antibiotics, force feedings, intravenous fluids, heating blankets, oxygen support, and other general assistance. Occasionally blood transfusions are needed if the red blood cell count drops below 15 percent.

I have several patients who are FIV positive and lead fairly normal lives. Because their resistance is lowered, however, it's important not to stress them or subject them to any unnecessary traumas, weather conditions, vaccines, or other stressful factors. I insist that the owners keep these cats indoors so they cannot spread the disease to other cats. If they fall ill for any reason, it is important to get veterinary help early on so treatment can be started immediately. Any delay can usher on the demise of the kitten. It's always a roller-coaster of a life—good days and bad. You should be prepared for this if your kitten is diagnosed with FIV.

Diagnosis of FIV is made using a blood test that's better than 90 percent accurate. For a period of several weeks following infection, the test doesn't turn up positive—called a window of "false negative" test result. If the disease is expected and one negative test result comes back from the lab, a second test should be taken 4 to 6 weeks later to confirm.

There is no cure for this disease, and no vaccine presently guards against it. Take necessary precautions to safeguard other cats in the household. Separate the positive kitten from the rest. Keep him indoors, and shower him with all the love you can.

Feline Infectious Peritonitis (FIP)

This is perhaps the most bizarre of all the feline diseases. FIP belongs to the coronavirus family, which include many viruses—mostly non-lethal intestinal viruses. The FIP strain is different. It occurs most often in multi-cat households. The virus is contagious through contact with the bodily fluids of infected cats, which can happen when cats share food and water dishes, or litter boxes.

Kittens can be born with FIP if the queen mother had it. This is one of the leading causes of infant death, or *Fading Kitten Syndrome*, where kittens die days after birth for no apparent reason. If the kitten contacts the virus later on, he will experience an initial period of illness during which the virus multiplies in the lymphatic system. Then the virus spreads to internal organs, where it causes inflammation and disease. High fevers of over 104°F are common. This is where things get strange. The FIP disease takes two forms (wet and dry forms), for which the symptoms can differ:

- **Wet.** "Wet," doesn't mean the cat looks or feels wet. "Wet" describes the internal situation. The FIP virus causes a leaking of blood fluids and serum out of the blood vessels, and into different organs, causing inflammation and fluid buildup. The organs affected most are spleen, liver, lung, brain, eyes, and lymph nodes. Body cavities, such as the chest and abdomen, also fill with fluid. The fluid often can be noted on a physical exam. These kittens breathe with difficulty, appear yellow from jaundice, are dehydrated, and are losing weight quickly. Most of these kittens die within weeks of respiratory and heart failure; or from seizures resulting from increased pressure of water on the brain.

- **Dry.** The dry form is similar to the wet form, except no fluids accumulate in the organs or body cavities. However, you still see the inflammation of the organs due to cellular infiltration. The dry form is more insidious and the kitten can live with it for months to years. The disease progresses more slowly because the inflammation is dry.

FIP is perhaps the most difficult of all the feline diseases to diagnose, because the blood test available isn't specific for the FIP strain of the coronavirus. In other words, if the FIP test comes back positive, your veterinarian can't be sure if your kitten has the FIP strain or one of the considerably milder intestinal corona viruses. This might seem like a moot point, but it isn't when you have a cattery of dozens of valuable breeding cats, or a household of beloved pets, and you can't tell who has the real FIP strain and who merely has a harmless stomach flu.

Your veterinarian can run other tests to help diagnose FIP, such as a total blood (serum) protein level, which often is elevated in FIP. These proteins often show a specific pattern on an *electrophoresis test,* for which some laboratories can screen. The bottom line is that diagnosing FIP with certainty is impossible without either biopsy specimens or autopsy analysis of the diseased organs. I also have had a laboratory run an analysis on fluid I've extracted from the abdomen of a kitten I suspect might have the wet form. Most veterinarians rely on the clinical presentation of the kitten and a high FIP test result before conclusively suspecting FIP.

The first step in preventing this terribly debilitating disease is to identify the infected cats. An adult cat who contracts the virus might successfully fight the disease and become a *carrier* (one who is positive, and contagious to other cats, but doesn't seem to show symptoms). We need to identify these cats and remove them from catteries and multi-cat households to halt the spread of this evasive disease.

A vaccine is available for FIP, administered intranasally and recommended for any kitten who lives in a multi-cat household, is used for breeding, or frequently goes to cat shows.

The Vaccine Schedule

Having read about the horrors that commonly afflict kittens, I probably don't need to remind you to concentrate on protecting against them. This section presents a typical vaccine schedule your veterinarian might use on your kitten.

The distemper vaccine (FVRCP-C) is a combination of Feline Rhinotracheitis, Feline Calicivirus, Feline Panleukopenia, and Chlamydia (Pneumonitis). Your veterinarian starts it while your kitten is young, usually around six weeks, and administers it every three weeks until the kitten reaches twelve weeks.

The kitten receives a rabies vaccination just once, as young as twelve to sixteen weeks of age.

Feline Leukemia and Feline Infectious Peritonitis vaccines are recommended for kittens who go outdoors or who live in multi-cat households, and can be started as young as twelve weeks of age. You should request an initial blood test before having the kitten vaccinated against these diseases. After all, if the kitten is already positive, vaccinating would be pointless.

A Typical Kitten Vaccine Schedule				
Age in Weeks	**FVRCP-C***	**Rabies****	**FeLV***	**FIP***
6 weeks	X			
9 weeks	X			
12 weeks	X		X	X
16 weeks		X	X	X

*These vaccines require an annual booster.

**This vaccine requires a booster every one, two, or three years depending on the vaccine used.

Does Vaccinating Pose Any Drawbacks?

By far, vaccines do more good than harm. A vaccine can be less than beneficial, however, in two circumstances:

- **Allergic reaction.** Allergic reactions are quite rare, but some kittens *are* allergic to vaccines (based on my experience, I would estimate that about 1 kitten in 500 is allergic). A kitten could have an allergic reaction within twenty minutes of getting a vaccine. You might observe coughing, swollen face, drooling, and/or vomiting, as well as wheezing. If you notice any of these symptoms shortly following a vaccination, take the kitten back to your veterinarian right away so he or she can give antihistamine and cortisone drugs to counteract the reaction.

- **Vaccine-induced sarcoma.** A growing body of evidence indicates that a very small percentage of cats and kittens who receive conventional FDA-approved feline vaccines will develop a certain malignant type of cancer (called *fibrosarcoma*) of the subcutaneous tissues at the injection site months to years later. The good news is that it doesn't tend to spread. The bad news is that it can be difficult to remove and tends to return even when you do successfully remove it. The vaccines with which these sarcomas are most often associated are the rabies and feline leukemia vaccines (the killed type vaccines).

The important thing to keep in mind is that the risk of getting the diseases that these vaccines aim to prevent generally far outweighs the risk of getting a sarcoma tumor from the vaccine. Studies have shown that up to one-third of cats who go outside regularly have a high risk of contracting feline leukemia, and many states mandate rabies vaccines for public health reasons. Ask your veterinarian for an opinion on this matter and how best to vaccinate your kitten. If your kitten should develop a vaccine-induced tumor, ask about available treatment options, such as surgery to remove the bulk of the tumor, followed up with radiation treatments or chemotherapy.

Basic Screening Blood Tests

During one of your first visits, your veterinarian probably will recommend testing your kitten's blood for the most common kitten diseases. Your kitten could already have caught a disease from an infected cat at the breeder's, shelter, pet store, or rescue society, or might have been born with one if his mother had it during her pregnancy. You might want know whether your kitten is infectious for several reasons:

- You have other cats at home you want to keep from getting infected

- You have a health guarantee from the breeder or pet store
- You simply want to ensure you have a healthy kitten

The three most common blood tests are as follows:

- Feline Leukemia (FeLV) test
- Feline Immunodeficiency Virus (FIV) test
- Feline Infectious Peritonitis (FIP) test

These tests can all be performed from one blood sample, and often right in the veterinarian's office. For a complete discussion of these diseases, see the section on the diseases which we vaccinate for earlier in this chapter.

The problem arises when one or more of these tests shows positive. Just because your kitten has a positive test result doesn't mean you have to do anything drastic. I don't encourage euthanizing a kitten unless it's terminally ill. Many people keep their kittens for years under strict guidance from their veterinarian. A veterinarian can tell you how to properly care for a kitten who has a serious viral disease. You also should be advised that your kitten isn't normal and probably won't live out his usual lifespan.

What Does a Positive Test Result Mean?

- Your kitten was infected in utero (in the uterus) or shortly after birth
- Your kitten never really will be completely healthy and could need special care
- Your kitten might not live a normal life span
- Your veterinarian should repeat the test to make sure there was no mistake

The Physical Exam

Perhaps the most important part of the first visit to the veterinarian is the physical exam. It is crucial for getting your kitten off on the right paw. It is during this exam that your veterinarian checks for your kitten's health status and birth defects.

A physical exam is systematic and should evaluate all the major organ systems. It also includes taking a temperature and looking for a fever. Let's go through each organ system briefly to demonstrate what your veterinarian is looking for.

- **Eyes.** Eyes should be clear of discharge or redness, and not swollen. Your vet checks for cataracts and birth defects of the retina.

- **Ears.** Ears should be clean and free of debris. Your vet checks for ear mites, which are common mites that live in kitten's ears. White kittens should be checked for deafness, as they are genetically susceptible.

- **Nose and throat.** There should be no sneezing or discharge from the nose. A yellow discharge usually indicates an upper respiratory infection. The throat should not be red or have any raised swellings or plaques, which can indicate viral infection. The vet checks for cleft palate, which is a hole in the roof of the mouth of a young kitten.

- **Heart and lungs.** Your veterinarian makes sure the lungs are clear and there is no heart murmur. The lungs should have no wheezing or wet sounds. There should be no heart arrhythmia (irregular beating).

- **Skin and coat.** The coat should be shiny and soft, without patches of hair loss or crusting. The veterinarian checks for evidence of external parasites, like fleas or mange mites. The skin should have a normal texture and elasticity. If not, it could indicate a disease or skin.

- **Abdomen.** The abdomen shouldn't be pendulous or bloated, which can indicate internal parasites like roundworms or coccidia. There shouldn't be any hernias, especially at the bellybutton, which is an *umbilical hernia*. The kitten shouldn't be constipated or painful in the abdomen. Your vet checks for hardness or tension in the abdomen, as well as the presence of all the internal organs—kidneys, liver, spleen, urinary bladder, and intestines.

- **Muscles and skeleton.** The vet checks the entire skeletal system for deformities or disease. Kittens can be born with angular deformities of the legs, which means the bones are not straight and have a curvature. The vet also checks for *dwarfism*, which occurs in the Munchkin breed cats. The spine should have no curvature, and the neck and tail should be straight, not kinked. The kitten shouldn't have muscle cramping or spasms.

- **Genitals.** The vet checks the male or female genitals for normal structure and size. Some males are born with none, or only one testicle, called *cryptorchid*, which means they aren't suitable for breeding. These kittens' testicles may descend until up to 12 weeks of age, but they still should be neutered. Females should have a small vulva without discharge. A kitten with male and female sexual organs is called a *hermaphrodite*.

- **Lymph nodes.** These are the glands located under the neck, armpits, groin, and behind the knees. If these glands are enlarged or painful, it usually signifies an infection. These kittens should be tested for the various aforementioned viral diseases.

- **Neurology.** The vet checks the kitten for basic reflexes, including pupillary of the eye, facial nerves, inner ear (for balance), knee jerk, and anal tone. The vet also should check the kitten for *cerebellar hypoplasia*, a condition in which the kitten has no coordination and shakes constantly.

Worming and Intestinal Parasites

Checking for worms is an integral part of your kitten's first vet visit. Studies have shown that up to 80 percent of all kittens are born with worms. What kind of worms? The following sections discuss the several different species that can infect kittens.

The first thing your veterinarian will want to do is run a fecal (stool) exam on your kitten, so bring a sample with you. The procedure takes only ten minutes to run, so you often can get a result before the end of appointment. Don't be surprised if it comes back positive.

Roundworms (Ascarid)

Roundworms are perhaps the most common of all kitten worms. The worm is *Toxocara cati*, spaghetti-like worms that are several inches long. They inhabit the stomach and small intestines.

They rob the kitten of food because they compete for food material in the intestines and stomach. They cause bloating of the abdomen, smelly, loose stools, flatulence, and vomiting. In fact, some kittens vomit up adult worms. Because the worms take food, most infected kittens are always hungry. They have a classic appearance: bloated abdomen but thin, with ribs, spine, and hip bones protruding. These kittens might also have pale mucous membranes and be anemic from malnutrition.

The life cycle of a roundworm is relatively simple. Adult roundworms inhabit the stomach and intestines of cats, where they feed and lay eggs. These eggs either pass out with the stool where they become infective for other cats, or they hatch and release larvae within the intestine, which migrate through the body and can end up in organs, mammary glands, or back in the intestine. This whole process takes about three weeks. Therefore, a kitten can become infected with roundworms by either ingesting stool that contains eggs or nursing on an infected mother (thereby ingesting larvae in the milk). The latter is the most common.

Your veterinarian diagnoses roundworms in your kitten based on the kitten's

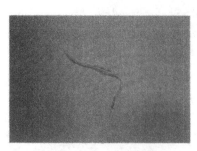

Close-up of a roundworm.

appearance, seeing roundworms in the stool or vomit, or a microscopic fecal examination that shows the eggs.

Treatment is easy with new anthelmintic drugs that kill parasites. The most common wormer used for roundworms in kittens is Pyrantel pamoate. It kills only adults, however, so it needs to be given twice, about three weeks apart (that's how long it takes larvae to mature into adults). There is a new wormer on the market that only needs one dose, and kills all intestinal worms of cats.

Kittens infected with roundworms have bloated
abdomens, like this one.

Roundworms can infect people, especially children. They are transmitted *fecal-orally*, meaning, the person or child must put infected cat feces, or fecal-contaminated soil, into their mouth. The thought is horrifying, but the fact is, young children do these things. A common scenario involves children playing in a sandbox that cats use as a litter box.

The problem that occurs when roundworms infect people is that once the larvae hatch from the eggs in the stomach and small intestine, they get lost trying to find their way. Lost larvae wind up in the strangest places, such as the liver, kidney, brain, and eye. Their presence alone in these organs commonly results in damage. Ascarid larvae in people is called *Visceral Larva Migrans*. This should be a serious consideration to all families who have young children who have a kitten with roundworms.

Hookworms (Ancylostoma)

Hookworms are another type of worm that can infect your kitten. Rather than feed off food substance in the intestine, like roundworms, hookworms latch onto the gut lining with their three teeth and suck blood. Affected kittens can present with bloated abdomens, but the most striking symptom is anemia, or loss of red blood cells. These kittens have pale mucous membranes of the mouth and generally are weak.

A kitten can become infected with hookworms in the following four ways:

- Ingesting feces that contain hookworm eggs
- Inheriting them from a mother queen in utero (in the uterus) during pregnancy

- Ingesting them through the queen's milk during nursing, because the mother sheds larvae in her milk
- The hookworm larvae actually burrowing right through the kitten's skin (the "dermal route")

The life cycle, diagnosis, and treatment are similar to roundworms.

Like roundworms, hookworms pose a threat to people, especially children. The larvae of the hookworm can burrow through tender foot skin. As children run barefoot in a contaminated yard, the hookworm larvae can invade their skin; a condition called *Cutaneous Larva Migrans*. These larvae easily become confused and get lost trying to find their normal migration route through the lungs. In children, the larvae migrate through the skin. The larvae cause red, raised serpentine eruptions of the skin that are intensely itchy. You can actually see the worms under the skin! Luckily for us, the skin is a dead end for these larvae. They usually go no further, but can cause an allergic reaction. Hookworms pose more of a threat in the warm climates of the Southeast region of the United States, but I have seen a case in New York. The classic scenario, again, entails the family cat using the kids' sandbox as a large litter box. If the feces of the cat are contaminated with hookworm eggs, the children are at risk.

The treatment for hookworms is the same as for roundworms.

Tapeworms (Cestodes)

Tapeworms are very common in kittens. Tapeworms are flat, white, ribbon-like, half-inch-long segmented worms that live in the small intestines of animals. They break off in segments that move and often wiggle right out of the

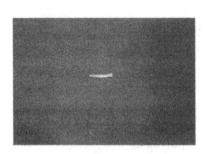

A tapeworm segment.

kitten's rectum! Many owners are horrified to see these segments, which look just like grains of rice on the kitten's stools—moving. As you can imagine, this quickly prompts a call to the vet's office. The good news is that they are basically harmless to the kitten except for some intestinal cramping, rectal itching, and abdominal distention. If the kitten has a heavy infestation, however, it can lose weight and appear emaciated.

The life cycle is complicated and involves rodents and fleas. The kitten can get tapeworms in the following two ways:

- By having fleas, and ingesting them while grooming
- By eating infected rodents

Diagnosis is easy because you can actually see these worms. In fact, they don't show up on regular fecal exams very often. Treatment is even easier these days with anti-cestode drugs, usually given once as a tablet.

Coccidia

Coccidia isn't a worm, it's a protozoa (like an amoeba)—a single-celled organism that lives in the small intestines of animals. Coccidia are very common in barnyard animals and cats. In large populations, these parasites cause intestinal bloating, diarrhea, bloody stools, flatulence, weight loss, and straining to defecate.

The vet diagnoses coccidia by doing a fecal test. The *cysts*, or eggs, of the protozoan are easily identified under microscopic examination. Your veterinarian can treat your kitten with a sulfonamide antibiotic to kill the coccidia. Treatment usually is for 5–10 days, depending on the severity.

Giardia

Giardia is another protozoan that lives freely in natural water sources like streams, ponds, and lakes. Most wild animals have giardia because they drink from these water sources and become infected. People who don't boil outdoor water before drinking also are at risk of getting giardia. In people, the disease is a dysentery-like diarrhea. Kittens become infected with giardia by drinking outdoor water or eating wild animals that are infected.

In kittens, the disease also manifests as a dysentery-like bowel disease, including mucusy stools, diarrhea, abdominal cramping, and loss of appetite. Rarely do you see blood. Many kittens become resistant to this parasite and can live for years without a relapse. A small percentage of kittens do require treatment, however.

Diagnosis is made by identifying the giardia protozoan or its cysts (eggs) in the stool, best done by taking a direct rectal smear and examining it immediately under the microscope. Newer antigen tests, which are very sensitive, can now detect very small numbers of parasites in the feces. This is very useful because giardia often proves elusive and can infect in small numbers, making it hard to diagnose.

Treatment of giardia is anti-protozoan drugs. One of the most popular of these is Metronidazole. These drugs usually are used for only five days owing to possible side effects. *People are also at risk of getting giardia, but usually from drinking the same infected water, not directly from the kitten. Consult your physician with your health concerns.*

Toxoplasmosis

This parasite also is a protozoan. Widespread in the feral animal populations, it easily infects cats who hunt and eat raw meat. After a cat eats infected raw meat, such as a mouse, the parasites disperse into muscle and brain tissue, where they often remain without causing disease in a healthy cat. The problem results because the cat's feces contain *oocysts* (eggs) of the parasite, which are infective for other cats and people.

The vet makes a diagnosis based on one of two conditions:

- Finding oocysts in the feces
- Discovering antibodies to toxoplasma, via a blood test that measures antibody levels, called a *titer*

Treating toxoplasmosis can be difficult. In my experience it can take weeks or months of sulfur antibiotics to bring the titer down to negative or reach a point where no oocysts appear in the stool.

Toxoplasmosis is a major health concern for pregnant women, causing birth defects in the developing fetus. Another source of toxoplasmosis is raw or undercooked meat. The American Animal Hospital Association has a list of guidelines for people who might be planning a family and have cats with toxoplasmosis. You definitely should consult your own physician for further information.

Preventing Toxoplasmosis in Your Home

- Someone other than the pregnant woman should clean the litter box, because the toxoplasmosis oocysts live in cat's feces.
- The litter box should be changed at least every 24 hours, because the feces don't become infective until after sitting in the litter box for 36–48 hours.
- Wear rubber gloves when cleaning the litter box and wash your hands thoroughly afterwards. Avoid inhaling dust from the litter box.
- Only feed your cat dry food or commercially prepared canned food, never raw or undercooked meat. Try to keep them from hunting rodents.
- Ask your physician about other steps you can take to avoid getting this disease during your pregnancy. Some physicians recommend a blood test for toxoplasmosis for women who have cats.
- You might need to ask a family member or a friend to keep your cat during your pregnancy if your physician insists that the cat not live in the house.

Chapter 3

Kitten Health Maintenance

Now that you've cleared the first hurdles and taken your first trip to the vet, you're ready to learn about basic health maintenance. This chapter covers the following topics:

- Grooming
- Keeping eyes, ears, and teeth healthy
- Declawing (the pros and cons)
- Administering medicines
- Handling your kitten
- Spaying and neutering

Grooming

Grooming is vital to keeping your kitten healthy, especially if your kitten is long-haired. Think of the coat as the fur and skin together: You can't have a healthy coat unless both the skin and fur are healthy.

Cats naturally maintain well-groomed coats. Look at your kitten's tongue—notice the bristles facing backward. Cats use these bristles to groom themselves, often beginning to do so as young as several weeks of age. They methodically lick their coat, usually in one direction, often for hours at a time.

As much as kittens do for themselves, they do sometimes need your help. Your kitten's tongue can't reach certain areas—like behind the ears and on top of their head and back. Also, their little bristles can't always get through a tough mat of hair. That's where you come in.

Grooming is necessary for all cats, regardless of the length of their coats. Long-haired cats in particular, however, call for a few special considerations. This section in no way substitutes for a good groomer, but it does educate you concerning what you can do at home between trips to the groomer.

The Benefits of Regular Grooming

- Removes dead and unwanted hair and skin flakes or dandruff
- Lets the skin breath, promoting good skin health
- Exposes skin disease and parasites more quickly
- Spreads natural skin oils and adds luster to coat
- Makes the kitten feel good
- Gets your kitten used to handling and encourages bonding

The Coat

From birth to about twelve weeks of age, your kitten has an *immature coat*—the fur is fluffy and almost feathery in texture. At around twelve weeks of age, your kitten's adult coat begins to grow. The adult coat is coarser and longer than kitten fur. Most kittens have an *undercoat*, a downy layer of insulating fur that lies between the skin and the outer layer, or over coat. The undercoat conserves body heat and helps maintain body temperature. It constantly replenishes itself by shedding the older hairs and growing new ones.

The overcoat is what you see and feel when you run your hand over his body, and which acts as the protective layer that waterproofs and shields the skin from the elements.

Both the undercoat and overcoat shed regularly. Cats who live in regions that have seasonal temperature and daylight changes usually shed twice a year—in spring, to shed out the old winter coat, and again in the fall, to make way for a new winter coat. Cats who live indoors shed continually, but more slowly, all year long. Most grooming problems occur during the heavy shedding seasons, because the hair is turning over and coming out in fistfuls. The coat also is prone to matting and clumping during this time.

Conditions that can accelerate or increase shedding, other than seasonal changes, include nervousness or stress (short-term more than long-term), like trips to the vet; malnutrition or vitamin and mineral deficiencies; hormonal changes, such as a queen in heat; allergies and contact irritations; external and internal parasites; genetic baldness (Sphynx breed); and skin diseases, like bacterial and fungal infections.

The coat and skin are living organs, so they have certain nutritional needs. The skin needs certain levels of nutrients (vitamins, minerals, proteins, and fats), as well as water, to keep it in top form. Protein is the building block of skin and hair, and the important vitamins for the coat are A, B, and E. Zinc is a necessary mineral, as well. The coat also requires fats and fatty acids to remain oiled and moisturized.

Grooming Basics

Grooming a cat—short- or long-haired—consists of five basic steps:

1. Brushing and combing
2. Dematting
3. Shampooing
4. Blow drying and brush-outs
5. Trimming nails

Each step requires a bit of work and patience. I discuss each one in turn so you can follow along at home. But before we begin, I want to clarify a few points. I'm addressing these guidelines to the amateur; they're just tips and do not substitute for a professional groomer. Sometimes you can't do it yourself and need professional assistance, especially if you have a long-haired cat that mats badly, or a cat who becomes violent during grooming. You also might want to read the section on holding your kitten, "Handle with Kit Gloves," later in this chapter. As you can imagine, kittens don't generally like water and can require special handling. Some cats object so strenuously to bathing that you need to sedate them. If that's the case with your pet, do not let your groomer do it—let only licensed veterinarians give your animal sedatives of any kind. Your kitten shouldn't need a grooming until at least 14–16 weeks of age.

Tools of the Trade

The following list explains the basic tools you need for proper kitten and cat grooming. They're slightly different than the ones used on dogs, being generally smaller, and designed for the silkier fur of cats. In other words, if you also have a dog and have some grooming tools for him, don't assume you can use them on your kitten.

- **Brushes.** Several different types of brushes are available for pets. Most of them are wired slicker types with wire bristles or pin brushes with rounded tips. I like the pin brushes because they're gentler on the skin and don't scratch or hurt. Boar's hair bristle brushes also are good for spreading oils, but just like the slicker brushes, they only skim the surface of the coat and fail to get deep enough to remove undercoat. Think of brushes as good for luster and making the hair lay flat.

- **Specialty Brushes.** A variety of specialty tools are available for grooming cats. You use these to remove excess fur and scaling, crusting, or dead skin. They have rubber knobs that are effective, but gentle on the skin. They come in a variety of handheld styles or in a mitt or glove that has the rubber knobbies on the palm. These also work great during the bath to remove the wet undercoat.

- **Combs.** Combs usually are made of stainless steel or plastic. I prefer stainless steel combs because you can disinfect them, they never break, and they come in a variety of tooth separations—from fine fleacombs (the teeth are so close they snag out fleas) to coarser, widetoothed combs for pulling out mats. You use combs to get deeper into the coat and remove the dead hair and undercoat. Some combs are half fine teeth and half coarse teeth. Some combs have rotating pins for easier glide through the coat, which comes in handy for long-haired cats.

- **Dematting combs.** Specialized combs for slicing through mats of fur, usually featuring sharp blades that you pull through the matted hair, cutting it into smaller pieces that you then can more easily comb out using a stainless steel. comb. The groomer holds the dematting comb with the blades pointed toward herself and draws it through the mat towards herself, being careful not to cut her thumb.

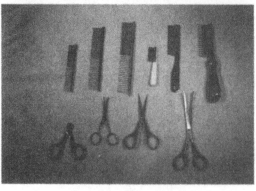

Assorted grooming tools: a variety of scissors, combs, brushes and grooming mitts.

- **Scissors.** Scissors come in a variety of sizes, shapes, and curvatures, ranging from as short as three inches to as long as one foot. You use scissors to trim the long hairs of the overcoat. You can even get thinning shears, which just thin out the coat. Longer shears are good for creating long flowing lines, whereas curved and short shears are good for tight spots, like on the face, paws, and neck.

- **Clippers.** Electric clippers that have stainless steel blades can shave right through even the toughest mats. Some blades cut so that long hairs are left long, while others shave right down to the skin. The different clipper blades have numbers corresponding to the closeness of cut. Table 3.1 lists examples of various blades.
- **Nail Clippers.** The finale of a thorough grooming is trimming the nails. There is a special nail clipper designed specifically for cat nails. Dog nail clippers are too cumbersome and splinter cat's nails.

Table 3.1 Clipper Blades and Their Uses		
Blade Size	**Hair Length**	**Uses in Grooming**
4	5/8″	Leaves a fuller coat on body
5	1/2″	Leaves a fuller coat on body
7	1/4″	Good for clipping toplines
8½	3/32″	A popular body blade
10	1/16″	Used on faces, head, and close body
15	1/32″	Used on faces, head, and close body
30	1/64″	Cuts close for feet and groin
40	1/130″	Used to prep for surgery
5/8	1/32″	Narrow blade for feet
7/8	1/32″	Narrow blade for feet
8/8	1/32″	Narrow blade for feet

The beauty of electric clippers is that enable you to shave evenly, quickly, and as close to the skin as necessary to remove a close mat without cutting the skin. I often see kittens in my office with lacerations caused by owners trying to use scissors to cut out a mat. Clippers also cut evenly without the choppiness of scissors. On the other hand, some groomers say you can't get the same precision or control using clippers as you can using scissors. Also, clippers make a humming noise that frightens some cats. Be very careful of using electric appliances near water.

Brushing and Combing

Before water ever touches your kitten's coat, you need to brush and comb out all dead undercoat and remove all matted hair—the dead hair is fairly simple to remove when it's dry but becomes very difficult when wet. Use your stainless steel combs to comb out the dead hair. If you snag a mat, try combing it out first. If it's too big or too close to the skin, then use your electric clippers to shave it out. *Do not use your scissors, because you can inadvertently cut the thin skin.* Keep the mat pulled away from the skin, and keep the clipper blade parallel to the skin to avoid giving the skin *clipper burn* (chafing that results from shaving the clipper blade too close to the skin). Do small, overlapping sections so you don't miss any areas. Your kitten might not let you comb out the whole coat during just one sitting. You might have to do it in shifts. After, and only after, you remove all the dead hair and mats, have you adequately prepared the kitten for its bath.

Bathing

Bathing can be an easy task or a major ordeal, depending on your kitten's disposition toward water. Don't be shocked if your kitten hates water and panics at the sound of spraying water—most kittens do. They also aren't especially fond of the slippery footing afforded by most bath tubs and sinks. Why don't I just come out and say it—most kittens *hate* baths! Unless you have a very placid kitten, like a sedate Persian, you might need to consult the final section in this chapter, "Handling with Kit Gloves." Wearing leather gloves is a good start. You also might want to trim his nails before you bathe him (instructions later in this section).

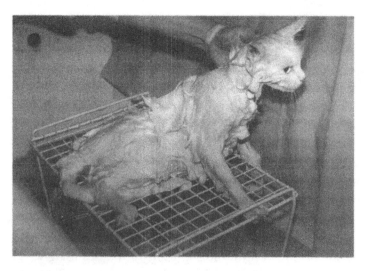

This kitten is getting a bath. Notice the grate that the groomer is using in the sink. It keeps the kitten from slipping. *Pam Koerner*

Professional groomers use a grating in the bottom of the tub or sink. You could use an old window screen. These grates, or screens, give the kitten something to grip with their nails during the bath. You also could use an old piece of carpeting. If you don't use something, don't be surprised if your kitten literally scrambles up the walls of the sink to get out.

Shampooing is next. First wet the fur. As mentioned, some kittens don't like the hissing sound of spraying water. To circumvent this situation, you can pre-fill buckets of warm water to pour over your kitten rather than spray him. Make sure you have enough water to wet the coat and then rinse thoroughly after you shampoo.

Selecting an appropriate shampoo can be confusing. Some shampoos formulated for kittens are gentle for sensitive kitten skin, pH-balanced for fur, and contain ingredients to moisturize, detangle, whiten, or kill bugs. Medicinal shampoos are available for skin infections, skunk odor, mold growth in the coat, seborrhea, anti-itch, and general dermatitis. If your kitten has a skin condition, your veterinarian can recommend a shampoo.

Regardless of the shampoo's specific purpose, always read the labels for instructions. Never get any shampoo in the kitten's eyes—it stings. Most groomers use a drop of mineral oil in each eye before shampooing to keep the soap out. Your veterinarian can give you an ophthalmic ointment to use, which might be better.

Start shampooing at the head and work your way back. Lather until you have soap suds everywhere except on the face. If you use an insecticide or medicinal ingredient, you will need to let the shampoo sit for the specified time. Get into every nook and cranny: between toes, under the tail, and in the groin area.

After you give the shampoo time to do its magic, it's time to rinse. Again, if spraying water gives your kitten paroxysms of fear, use buckets of warm water to pour gently over him. Rinse thoroughly until no soap residue remains. You can feel when the water rinses clean off the coat. Use your hands to wipe excess water from the coat, and be sure to go with the grain.

Now is the time to apply any coat conditioners, detanglers, moisturizers, or insecticide dips. Again, always follow directions. Towel dry your kitten with at least two dry towels. You might want to use chamois cloths, which absorb more water than a regular towel. After you towel him off, his coat should only be damp, not dripping wet. At this point, you need to brush out the coat.

Brushing Out

Brushing out your kitten involves using a handheld hair dryer and a brush. The intent of a good brush-out is to dry the coat down to the skin and remove any remaining dead fur. Hold the hand dryer about twelve inches away from

The final touches: brushing and blow-drying.

your kitten. Make sure the temperature setting is on low so that it doesn't burn the kitten's skin or your hand. Keep moving the dryer to different areas; don't stay on one spot too long. Use your brush *against the grain* to remove any remaining dead hair. Again, begin at the head and work your way down to the tail. Don't forget to dry the underbelly and between the hind legs. The blow-drying process can take up to 30 minutes for a long-haired cat.

Cutting Nails

Cutting your kitten's nails is the final stage of grooming. Most outdoor kittens rely on their nails, so you don't generally trim them. Most indoor kittens don't need their nails and often sharpen them on rugs, upholstery, and other furniture. You should trim indoor kittens' nails regularly to reduce the destruction to your furniture and to prevent them from catching or snagging on rugs.

The only part of the sharp, clear nail that you can trim is the point. The rest of the nail is supplied with nerves and blood vessels (called the *quick*), which means that if you cut too short (you may have heard the phrase, "cut to the quick"), it hurts and bleeds. You don't want that! So, let me tell you how to properly trim the nails. Hold the trimmer parallel to the base of the nail. You need to press on the toe pad to push the nail out of its normal retracted position. Look for the pink quick and *stay away from it*. Only trim off the clear tip. Do one nail at a time on one paw. If your kitten should jump and you accidentally cut into the quick, it bleeds. You can use a styptic pencil or push the bleeding end into a bar of soap to stop the bleeding.

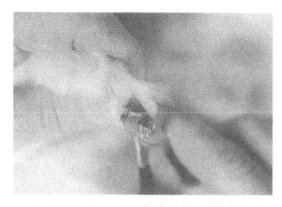

Use a clipper specially designed for cat nails (above); the trimmed nail (below).

Special Grooming Problems

Unusual circumstances which require special grooming techniques sometimes arise, and they usually involve removing a foreign substance from the fur.

Oil and Grease

Most kittens know to keep out of messy stuff like grease. Unfortunately, they can't always avoid these messes, such as when they walk across greasy countertops. You can easily remove most oils by using a degreasing agent or soap, or even a regular kitten shampoo. For stubborn oils slicks, you can use a phosphorous-free dishwashing detergent that contains very concentrated degreasing agents. Apply a spot no bigger than a dime directly to the oily spot. Rinse thoroughly until you feel no soap residue.

Burrs, Gum, Tar, and Other Sticky Stuff

Most sticky stuff gets hopelessly imbedded in a cat's fur. First, try to comb out the offending substance and, if that doesn't work, try softening it with mineral oil. Rub a small amount right into the sticky material, then try to comb it out. Don't despair if this doesn't work—you usually end up having to cut or shave off the clump, especially if it's close to the skin.

Fleas, Ticks, and Other Bugs

If you let your kitten outside during warm weather, you just might find little bugs crawling all over him when he comes back in. Chapter 7, "Skin Diseases," discusses allergic dermatitis and mange, and includes a complete discussion of fleas and ticks.

For now, however, let's just cover the basics of a flea and tick bath. Your first objective is to find a safe but effective flea and tick shampoo. Your veterinarian should be able to recommend one. The main concern is that the active ingredient (the insecticide that kills the bugs) be safe for kittens. Four types of active ingredients are commonly found in pet shampoos: organophosphates, pyrethrin, insect growth inhibitors, and citrus oils (see table 3.2).

If your kitten starts to act funny during the flea bath, he might be reacting to the insecticide in the shampoo, called *insecticide toxicity*. The first symptoms would be drooling and dilated pupils, which can then progress to twitching, vomiting, and disorientation. If you notice your kitten having a reaction, rinse him off immediately and thoroughly to eliminate all soap residue, then call your veterinarian for advice. Sometimes, your vet will need to administer a medication called *atropine*, which is the antidote to most insecticide reactions.

Skin Problems

A variety of shampoos is available for treating various skin afflictions. Your veterinarian or groomer should know which one you should use if your kitten has a skin problem. Table 3.3 offers some helpful tips on using medicated shampoos.

Skunk Spray

No one likes being sprayed by a skunk, especially your kitten. But it sometimes happens, and you need to deal with it immediately. The old home remedy of

Table 3.2   Insecticides in Pet Shampoos

Insecticide	Common Names	Effectiveness	Safety*	Signs of Toxicity	Treatment
Organo-phosphate	Carbryl, Malathion	extremely	no, often toxic	twitching, dilated pupils, hypersalivation	atropine injection, wash off
Pyrethrin	Pyrethrin, Allethrin	good, leave on for 5 minutes	generally safe, watch for skin irritations	skin irritations, excess salivation	atropine injection, wash off
Growth Inhibitor	Precor, Fenoxycarb	prevents eggs from hatching	yes	none	none
Citrus Oil	D-Limonene, Linalool	low, must leave on for 10 minutes	very safe, side effects rare	none	none

* Always follow label instructions

Table 3.3 Table of Medicated Shampoos			
Shampoo	**Active Ingredient**	**Uses**	**Actions**
Anti-Fungal	2% Miconazole	ringworm	kills fungus
Anti-Septic	Chlorhexiderm	bacterial dermatitis	anti-bacterial
Anti-Itch	Colloidal Oatmeal	allergic dermatitis	reduces itching
Anti-Seborrhea	Coal Tar	crusting and scaling	reduces skin flaking
Iodine	Iodine	infectious dermatitis	kills bacteria and fungus

tomato juice does carry some validity. Acidic juices, such as those of tomatoes and lemons, seem to neutralize the skunk odor. You also can obtain commercially prepared shampoos that neutralize the odor. Whatever you use, it can easily take two or three shampooings before you notice a reduction in stench. Even after that, on damp days you still might smell the lingering skunk aroma. Months can pass before it completely dissipates. Check to see if the eyes were affected, as this requires medical attention.

Stud Tail

Stud tail is peculiar only to male cats. Tom cats (intact males) have oil glands located at the base of their tail. These glands secrete an oil which the cat uses to spread, or preen, over his coat. You generally don't see this until the tom reaches sexual maturity around 6–8 months of age. If you bathe your kitten, you can use phosphorous-free dishwashing detergent as a degreasing agent. You can use talcum powder to absorb the excess oil between baths. Let the powder absorb overnight, then brush out the following day.

Eye Care

Many people consider eye care part of grooming. Actually, it's a bit more involved than just wiping out the corners of the eye with cotton after a bath. The eyes are sensitive and complicated organs. Kittens' eyes are particularly sensitive to airborne pollution, fumes, dust, and disease. The best thing you can do for your kitten's eyes is to keep them clean and minimize the irritations and exposure to disease. Long-haired kittens have a particular problem of getting hair in their eyes. Your groomer should be able to trim the hair so it doesn't get into the eyes and irritate them.

Keeping Eyes Bright

- Keep the hair trimmed short around the eyes to keep the eyes clear.

- Most kittens have dark brown dried tears in the corners of their eyes. Wipe them out with a damp wash cloth or sterile saline eye wash every morning.

- Never give your kitten any sharp-edged toys that could poke his eye.

- Be especially careful when grooming not to get any of the tools near the eyes, where they could cause injury.

- Keep your kitten out of areas in which dirty and dusty substances can get into their eyes.

- Don't keep kittens in areas heavy in construction debris or paint fumes.

- If redness or swelling develops, consult your veterinarian immediately—never delay in getting professional help when it involves the eyes.

Clear, bright eyes free of hair and irritants are more likely to stay healthy. The healthier the eyes, the more resistant they are to disease and infection. Let's look at a few things you can do to help. Diseases of the eyes are discussed later in Chapter 8, "Eye Diseases."

At some point in every kitten's life he will develop an eye problem. Please consult the kitten pediatric part of this book for the section on eye diseases for advice on what the condition may be. Don't wait more than a day to see your veterinarian if something is bothering the eyes. There is a good chance that he or she will prescribe eye medication, either in the form of ophthalmic drops or ointment. You will then have the job of applying the medication several times daily. Follow the directions in the section on giving medicine to your kitten.

Ear Care

Cats are fortunate in that most of them have erect ears (except for the Scottish Fold breed). An erect ear is one that stands up straight, allowing air and light to circulate in the ear canal. This is good. Light and air prevent certain pathogens from growing, like bacteria and yeast. This is why you see significantly fewer ear infections in cats than in dogs who have floppy ears.

To begin, let's examine the basic anatomy of an ear. On the outside, there is the ear flap, or *pinna*, a flap of cartilage sandwiched between two layers of skin. All ears are assembled the same, regardless of size, shape, or breed. At the junction of the pinna and the skull, the ear turns into a conical tunnel, called the *outer ear canal*. Two parts make up the outer ear canal: the vertical and horizontal canals. Think of the ear canal as an inverted letter "L." At the bottom of the horizontal canal lies the tympanic membrane, or ear drum, which separates the outer ear from the middle ear.

Routine Ear Cleaning

Cleaning out your kitten's external ear canal is part of regular grooming, and should be done with each bath. I'm talking about doing this at home following each grooming session. Use a commercially prepared ear cleaner. It should have a ceruminolytic agent to break up the wax. A few ear cleaners have antiseptic agents to discourage bacterial and yeast growth. You probably will discover that the market offers dozens of ear cleaners. Ask your vet which one is best for your kitten, or follow table 3.4.

Table 3.4　Which Type of Ear Cleaner to Use

Type of Problem	Surfactant (soap)	Ceruminolytic (dissolves wax)	Soothing Extract	Antiseptic Agents
Just Plain Dirty	X			
Waxy Ears	X	X		
Sour Odor, no Wax	X			X
Sour Odor & Wax	X	X		X
Clean but Red	X		X	
Bacterial Infection	X		X	X
Yeast Infection	X		X	X
Frequent baths				

Regardless of which cleaner you use, you still use the same technique. Follow these guidelines for cleaning:

1. Use cotton balls. *Never use cotton tipped swabs*, as these can damage the ear drum if improperly angled.

2. Moisten cotton with the ear cleaner.

3. Using your finger, gently swab the inside of the ear canal with the wet cotton.

4. Use circular motions to wipe out the ear canal.

5. If you notice an accumulation of dirt or wax, pour some cleaner into the ear canal, massage in with your hand, then rub off with dry cotton.

6. Continue until no more dirt comes out. It could take a dozen or more swabbings to clean a dirty ear.

7. Do the same for the other ear.

Ear Mites—The Most Common Ear Disease of Kittens

Ear mites are external parasitic microscopic bugs that live in the ear canals of animals. Kittens usually get ear mites from their mother during nursing as a newborn. The name of the ear mite is *Otodectes*, and they breed, colonize, and feed in the external ear canal.

As you can imagine, dozens of these bugs crawling around in an ear can be very itchy and irritating. Affected kittens scratch their ears until they bleed. The irritation from the mites also causes a dark brown waxy discharge in the ears. Your veterinarian can confirm the presence of the mites by using a magnified otoscope to look into the external ear canal. Some veterinarians will take a cotton swab and place some of the ear wax on a microscope slide so you can actually see these small mites.

Treating the mites is fairly simple. Years ago, people used to put mineral oil in the ear canals of kittens to kill the mites. This does work, but because the oil only smothers the mites, it takes weeks, and is very oily and messy. Nowadays, we use a two-step method that works quickly and with much less mess.

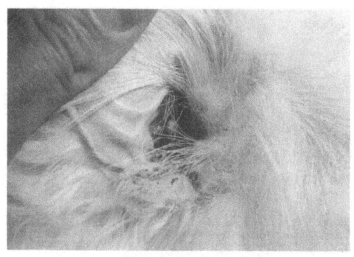

The black discharge on this ear is a sign of ear mites.

The first step is to thoroughly clean the ears, as described above. After you clear the ear canal of all wax debris, you apply an insecticidal lotion into the ears, massage it in, and then use a cotton ball to wipe out the excess. Depending on the lotion, you need to reapply it daily or weekly. You must treat both ears, even if you have found mites only in one, because they can migrate from one ear to the other. Applying a flea powder around the head and neck

Drawing of an ear mite.

area also kills the mites should they try to escape the ear, which they might do when you apply the lotion. You can expect severe cases of ear mites to take several weeks to completely treat.

Many vets are using a new treatment, although it isn't yet approved by the Food and Drug Administration for this purpose. The vet injects a highly effective *anthelmintic* (bug killing drug), called *ivermectin*, twice, one week apart. Your vet should still professionally clean the ears, but the anthelmintic injection eliminates the need for the lotion. I have used this treatment with great success, especially in severe cases, or those in which the owners cannot medicate the kitten at home for one reason or another.

Ear mites reportedly have infected people, but neither I nor any of my clients have experienced this. The human ear canal is shorter than an animal's, which leaves the mites looking for a more suitable host.

Dental Care

Kittens have teeth too! Most people overlook the need to maintain their kitten's teeth, but that's a mistake. Cats rely on their teeth as much as people

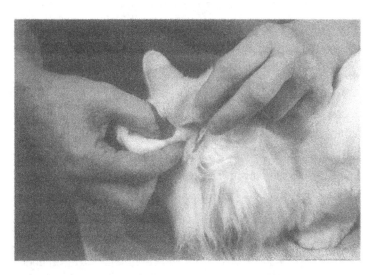

Here a veterinarian shows how to use a cotton ball to properly clean the ear.

do. Just stop for a minute and think about what people do to keep their teeth healthy. People brush and floss their teeth daily, often more. Many people use anti-plaque mouthwash, and regular dental visits.

Now just think what would happen if you did *nothing*. No brushing, no floss, no regular dental visits. How long do you think you'd keep your teeth? History informs us that people in years long gone who did little to nothing in the line of dental hygiene lost their teeth in early adulthood. The exact same thing happens to cats if you don't step in and start a dental maintenance program, early on. Let's start with information on cat's teeth.

Normal Teething and Dentition

Kittens go through two teething processes. When they're just babies, they start cutting their *deciduous* teeth—the teeth that come in between three and six weeks of age. These are all replaced with permanent adult teeth starting at 16 weeks and finishing between five and six months of age.

Normal Tooth Anatomy

Kittens have teeth just like us. They have incisors, canines, premolars, and molars. All of a kitten's teeth are made the same way, regardless of size or shape.

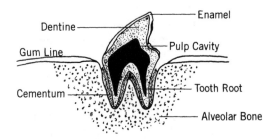

Drawing of a normal tooth. All are composed of the same elements regardless of their size or position in the mouth.

Glossary of Dental Terms

This section makes understanding the language of dentistry a bit easier. You will probably recognize some of the terms, while others will be new.

> **Alveolar bone.** The bone of the skull (for upper teeth), or jaw (for lower teeth), in which the roots of the teeth sit.
>
> **Caries (cavity).** The erosion and destruction of tooth enamel and dentine to cause a crater in the tooth, usually done by acid produced by bacteria in plaque and tartar.
>
> **Cementum.** The connective tissue that anchors the tooth root to its socket in the alveolar bone.
>
> **Crown.** The part of the tooth above the gum line (the part you can see), almost entirely covered by enamel.
>
> **Dentine.** The bulk of a tooth, found just below the enamel, and also hard, but not nearly as hard as the enamel. If the enamel cracks or erodes, the dentine becomes exposed to the air.

Enamel. The white or off-white hard substance that covers and protects the deeper structures of a tooth, and which gives a tooth its white color and high gloss. The hardest substance in the body.

Neckline lesion. A caries along the gum line, parallel with the gums.

Periodontal disease. (also known as *Periodontitis*). An inflammation of the tissues around and supporting the teeth, such as the gums, alveolar bone, and connective tissue. Usually starts from an accumulation of plaque and tartar between the crown of the tooth and surrounding tissues, causing a separation of the tooth and its socket, allowing bacteria and infection to further detach the tooth from its socket, eventually leading to tooth loss.

Plaque. A sticky film comprised of bacteria, saliva, white blood cells, and mineral deposits.

Pulp cavity. The sensitive center of a tooth, which contains the dental nerve, artery, and vein. This fleshy center has feeling and bleeds if disrupted.

Tartar (dental calculus). A hard yellow to grayish-green mineralized coating on teeth comprised of saliva, plaque, minerals, food particles, and bacteria. One of the main causes of periodontal disease.

Tooth abscess. A pocket of infection around the roots of a tooth and the alveolar socket, causing pain, swelling, bleeding, pus formation, and eventually tooth loss.

Tooth root. The finger-like projections at the base of a tooth that carry the dental nerve and blood vessels to the pulp cavity, seated into the alveolar bone.

Keeping That Smile Bright

You should follow the two following caveats to keep your kitten's teeth and gums healthy:

1. Your kitten's diet should be at least 50 percent dry food.

2. You must take steps to reduce the amount of plaque and tartar accumulation.

In Chapter 4, "Feeding and Nutrition," I give other reasons why dry food should comprise at least 50 percent of your kitten's total diet. So what else can you do? To remove plaque from your kitten's teeth before it hardens into tartar, start brushing his teeth at 5–6 months of age.

Brushing Your Kitten's Teeth

You should brush your kitten's teeth at least once a week. *If you introduce your kitten to this procedure early on, it won't be a struggle later in life.* If you want to be fancy, you can use commercially available cat toothpaste and tooth-brushes, but you can just as effectively use one of your old toothbrushes and baking soda. You can use small, rubber, knobby finger cots that you put over your finger to use as finger toothbrushes. Regardless of the instrument you prefer, be sure to add just enough water to two tablespoons of baking soda to make it pasty. Apply the paste to the head of the toothbrush or directly to the outer surfaces of the teeth. You must lift the lips to do this. The key is to start at the gum line and brush downward in a circular motion. Concentrate on the outer surfaces of the upper molars, because this is where most of the tartar and plaque accumulates. Brush vigorously for two minutes.

If your kitten gets tired sooner, take a short rest, then continue. You don't have to rinse. You can get away with brushing only once a week because in animals the plaque takes several days to mineralize into tartar in animals. Dentists tell us that our plaque needs only 24 hours to do that, hence the rule to brush at least once a day. Obviously, the more you brush, the healthier the teeth and gums will be.

You also can purchase hygiene sprays specially formulated to spray or swab onto your kitten's teeth daily. They help kill bacteria, neutralize odors, and some contain fluoride. Again, you don't have to rinse.

A *professional cleaning* is performed by a veterinarian and his or her staff. It involves using a combination of handscaling, as well as an ultrasonic unit which literally blasts tartar off. The process is a bit tedious and must be done

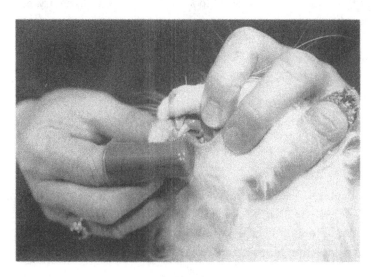

Using a finger tooth brush to brush kitten's teeth.

slowly. All surfaces must be scaled to remove even the smallest amount of tartar from all surfaces of the tooth. Each tooth is scaled separately. Once all teeth are done, they need to be polished with a tooth polisher (called a *prophy*). The reason is that during the scaling, microscopic lines are made in the enamel. If these aren't smoothed out by polishing, then they will provide a place for tartar to accumulate. Scaling is recommended when tartar is noted to accumulate on the teeth, or yearly as part of a prevention program.

Many veterinarians require anesthetizing your kitten using a general anesthetic during the scaling, so that they can get around each tooth and do a more thorough job. This is fine; however, be aware that an alternative to general anesthesia is available. I often use a heavy sedative, with which there are fewer health risks. Although this might seem awkward for the vet, and certainly takes more time and patience, the kitten isn't subjected to general anesthesia.

Following at least two or three of the preceding suggestions greatly increases your kitten's chances of keeping the beautiful set of teeth with which he was born for the duration of his life.

Spaying and Neutering

The vast majority of new kitten owners do want their kitten *spayed* (if it's a female) or *neutered* (if it's a male) to prevent the kitten from becoming sexually active. The average age at which we spay or neuter a kitten is six months, when they go through puberty and their sex hormones become active. Please keep in mind that both procedures are surgical, require general anesthesia, entail a recuperation period of a couple of weeks for the spay, a couple of days for the neuter, and must be performed by a veterinary surgeon.

Spaying

The spay procedure is a surgical *ovario-hysterectomy*, performed at 6 months of age. Spaying entails the surgical removal of both ovaries and the body of the uterus. To fully understand this, you must first know what these organs do, and where they are.

The *ovaries* are the female organs. They are suspended from the kidney by a ligament. They manufacture the eggs which are released during breeding. Most kitten queens have their first heat cycle at about 6–7 months of age (earlier in some cases). Cats in heat are very precocious, meow often, try to get outside, keep their tail raised and flick it, and seem restless or overly affectionate. The average heat cycle lasts 2 weeks.

Cats are *induced ovulators*, which means that the ovaries only release eggs for fertilization after breeding occurs. This makes breeding very efficient. The ovaries also secrete the female hormone, *estrogen*, which is required for proper

The Benefits of Spaying

- Removes the female hormone estrogen, preventing heat cycles and breeding
- Prevents pregnancy
- Prevents female medical diseases such as ovarian and uterine cancer
- Reduces the chances of mammary cancer
- Prevents unwanted kittens, which usually end up in overcrowded shelters

The Disadvantages of Spaying

- Increases the likelihood of weight gain, because it lowers the base metabolism
- Prohibits breeding or showing your queen
- Reduces activity level (some owners notice this, but not all)

development of the female reproductive tract and for the commencement of estrus. If you take away the ovaries, the queen has no eggs, and virtually no estrogen hormone, resulting in no heat cycles and infertility.

The *uterus* is the tubular organ that hosts the developing fetuses during pregnancy. Another name for the uterus is *womb*. The uterus is connected to the vagina by the *cervix*, a sphincter that opens and closes the passage into the uterus. When closed, the cervix keeps anything from entering the uterus. When open, it allows sperm to enter (during breeding), or fetuses to exit (during queening). Take away the uterus and cervix, and pregnancy becomes impossible.

You might be asking, "Why would I want to have my female kitten's uterus and ovaries removed? Nature put them there, why should I have them taken out?" The most obvious advantage is that she won't go into heat, and she can't breed or get pregnant. The following list summarizes the other advantages and disadvantages:

The risks of the anesthesia and surgery in general are low, but ask your vet about any special considerations regarding your kitten.

Neutering

Neutering is a euphemism for castration. When a veterinary surgeon neuters a male tom, he surgically removes the two testicles, leaving an empty scrotum.

The Benefits of Neutering

- Removes the male hormone *testosterone* from his system, thus preventing unwanted male behavior, such as spraying urine in the house (but must be done by 6 months of age to ensure behavioral effectiveness)
- Prevents male medical diseases like testicular cancer
- Most people find a neutered male a better house pet
- Prevents unwanted kittens that usually end up in overcrowded shelters

The Disadvantages of Neutering

- Increases likelihood of weight gain, because it lowers the metabolism
- Prohibits showing the cat in shows (other than in the neutered male category)
- Reduces activity level (claim some owners)

You should have a young tom neutered by six months of age if you want to reap the benefits of reducing male behavior.

The *testicles* are the male glands that manufacture sperm cells. Within the testicles are tubules (called *seminiferous tubules*) that produce sperm cells. The mature sperm cells are stored in a storage sack at the base of the testicle, called the *epididymis*. During *ejaculation*, sperm travels from the testicle, up the tube that leads into the abdomen (called the *spermatic cord*) and through the penis (via the *urethra*). The testicle hosts production of the hormone *testosterone*, which is responsible for male sexual characteristics, sexual performance, male physical characteristics, muscle size, and male behavior. Removing the testicles eliminates the testosterone. The testicles are housed in a skin pouch, called the *scrotum*, which serves not only as protection but also as a temperature controlling device. Neutering does leave the scrotum intact. The following list enumerates the advantages and disadvantages of neutering:

The risks of the anesthesia and surgery in general are low, but you should ask your vet about any special considerations regarding your kitten.

When and Why to Declaw

Declawing is a topic with which all veterinarians who treat kittens are faced. Let me say right off that a certain amount of controversy surrounds the

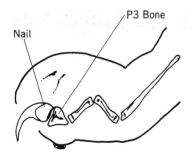

During declaw surgery, both the nail and the P3 bone are removed.

declawing issue. Some think that declawing a cat is an unnecessary alteration or mutilation, while others believe that it's a necessary part of having indoor cats.

My feeling is that cats are born with claws for a reason. Claws are an integral part of a cat's being and are as important to them as a good nose is to a dog. In all fairness, however, certain circumstances do arise in which declawing a kitten would be warranted. The most common being that he's destroying furniture—shredding drapes, furniture, and rugs. You might ask yourself, "Why not just trim his nails with a nail cutter?" Good question, but some kittens can make trimming their nails decidedly difficult, not to mention that it takes time. Declawing is a permanent solution. Done properly, the nails should never grow back. Follow these guidelines for who should be declawed and how their lives change.

Ask your veterinarian what he or she thinks about declawing. The only thing I can guarantee is that they will have an opinion. Find out about any special considerations regarding your kitten.

Guidelines for Declawing Kittens

- **Only declaw kittens over six months, but under 18 months of age.** Younger kittens naturally test their claws as part of growing up and might still outgrow their destructive tendencies; older kittens have become too dependent on them and it would be too much of a shock to remove them.

- **Only declaw kittens who will remain strictly indoors.** Kittens are defenseless against outside hazards without their front claws.

- **Only declaw kittens who have demonstrated consistent destructive behavior for at least two months.** It might just be a passing phase.

- **Only have the front claws declawed.** Never declaw all four paws because it renders the kitten completely defenseless if he should escape outside.

- **Allow the kitten to go through a period of adjustment after the declaw.** Some kittens become anxious or aggressive without their claws.

Giving Your Kitten Medicine

Somewhere along the line during your kitten's life, your veterinarian will send you home with medicine in one form or another. You will be responsible for administering it properly. All prescriptions that go out from a veterinary office are labeled with directions. These might sound easy enough, but just remember who you're dealing with—your wiggly, squirming, "I'd rather die than take that medicine" kitten.

The four basic types of medicines you might have to administer are as follows

Eye drops and ointments

Ear drops and ointments

Skin creams and ointments

Oral tablets, capsules, pastes, and liquids

You could encounter other forms of medicines, such as injections and suppository, but generally a trained professional administers these types.

I cover each of the preceding four basic types of medicine, describing proper technique. If your kitten is anxious or uncooperative, you might want or need a helper; also, consult the section "Handling with Kit Gloves," at the end of this chapter.

Eye Medication

Eye medicines usually come in the form of drops or ointment. Drops come in a small bottle and ointments usually come in a tube.

- **Drops.** To apply an eye drop to the eye, raise your kitten's nose upward about 45°. Gently pull up the upper eyelid so that the white of the eye is showing. Place one drop onto the white of the eye. Hold the nose up for ten seconds.

- **Ointment.** To apply ointment to the eye, raise your kitten's nose upward about 45°. Gently pull down the lower eyelid so that a pocket forms between the lower lid and the conjunctiva. Squeeze one-quarter inch of ointment into the pocket. Let go of the lower lid and allow the kitten to blink, which melts the ointment and spreads a thin layer evenly over the eye.

Ear Medication

Ear medicines usually come in drops or ointments, just like eye medicine. The difference is that they have to get into the ear canal.

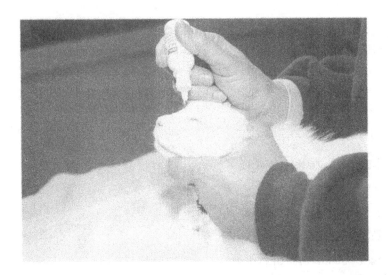

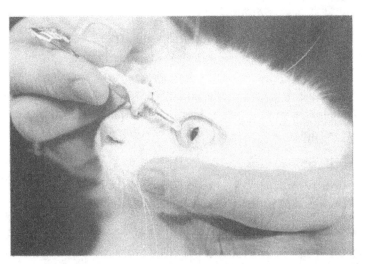

Should your kitten develop an eye problem, you'll
need to apply eye drops (upper) or ointment (lower).

- **Drops.** Tilt your kitten's head so that the ear receiving the medicine
  is up. Hold the ear flap so that you can see inside the ear canal. Place
  one or two drops so that it runs down the ear canal. Massage the base
  of the ear to evenly distribute the medication. Try to keep him from
  shaking his head for at least one minute to allow absorption.

- **Ointment.** Most ointment tubes come with a nozzle tip. Just like for
  drops, tilt the head and hold the ear flap. Insert the nozzle $\frac{1}{4}$ to $\frac{1}{2}$ inch
  into the ear canal and squeeze until the canal is filled (you should see
  the ointment welling back up). Then massage the base of the ear. Take
  a cotton ball and swab the excess ointment out of the ear canal.

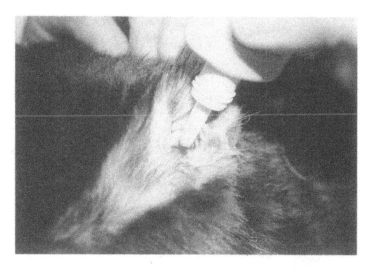

To put ear ointment in, hold the ear flap and squeeze the medicine into the ear canal.

Skin Medication

Skin medication usually takes the form of creams and ointments. You employ the same technique for both types. You need to rub creams evenly over the affected areas in a thin layer. Use a tissue or gauze square rather than your fingers. Don't leave too much on, or you're just inviting your kitten to lick it off. The best way to prevent licking is to cover the area, if possible. If you can't cover the cream, apply it just before feeding the kitten to distract him. If you can keep him from licking the cream off for five to ten minutes, most of it can be absorbed.

Oral Medication

Most oral medication comes in pills or capsules, pastes, and liquids. You give tablets and capsules the same way.

- **Tablets and capsules.** These are perhaps the most difficult for kittens to swallow. The best way to administer these is to point your kitten's nose upward toward the ceiling, to unlock the jaw. Using your third finger, push down on the lower jaw to open the mouth. Holding the pill with your first finger and thumb, drop the pill into the center of the back of the mouth, then quickly close the mouth and rub the throat or gently blow into the nose to stimulate swallowing. Then open the mouth again to make sure the kitten swallowed the pill. Don't be surprised if you see excess drool or even foaming at the mouth, especially if the medication is bitter. Note: Your veterinarian might have "pill guns," which keep your fingers out of your kitten's mouth. They can be

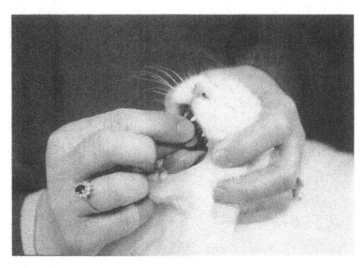

To give a pill, hold the mouth open and put the pill as far back in it as possible. Close the mouth and rub the throat to assist swallowing.

very handy to pill a cat, but your vet needs to show you the correct way to use it or you could end up choking your kitten.

- **Paste.** Pastes are usually either vitamin supplements or hairball laxatives. They come in tubes just like toothpaste. The best way to give a paste is to squeeze out the stipulated amount onto your first finger. Point your kitten's nose upward to unlock the jaw. With the mouth open slightly, stick the paste onto the roof of the mouth. The kitten has little choice but to swallow the paste, much like us getting peanut butter on the roof of our mouth. Don't be surprised if you see excess drooling or even foaming at the mouth, especially if the medication is bitter.

- **Liquid.** Liquids usually are the easiest medication to give orally to a cat. Draw up the appropriate amount of liquid medication into an eye dropper or a dosing syringe. *Do not try to open your kitten's mouth.* Just slide the tip of the dropper or syringe behind the upper fang (canine) tooth on one side, which makes him crack open his mouth. *Slowly* squirt the medication into the mouth so he can comfortably swallow it without choking. Rub the throat or blow in the nose to stimulate swallowing. Don't be surprised if you see excess drooling or even foaming at the mouth, especially with a bitter medication.

Taking Your Kitten's Temperature

As the parent of a young kitten or adult cat, you might occasionally need to take his temperature with a thermometer. If you call your veterinarian and say, "Doctor, I think my kitten has a fever!" don't be surprised if you get the

To effectively give liquid medicine, slide the syringe behind the upper fang and squirt slowly.

response, "What is his temperature?" You also might take your ill kitten to the vet and be sent home with instructions to take his temperature twice daily.

To take a kitten's temperature, you need a rectal thermometer. If you use a glass mercury thermometer, use a pediatric one. If you are buying one, I recommend the newer digital rectal thermometers for two reasons: the metal tip is smaller than the old mercury bulb ones, and the electronic ones get a reading in 30 seconds versus the two minutes or more required for the glass ones.

Regardless of the type of thermometer, you use the same technique. Apply a coating of petroleum jelly to the tip or bulb, and insert it into the rectum until the tip disappears. Leave the glass mercury ones in for two minutes. The electronic ones usually beep when they're done. Normal temperatures for kittens run in the 101–102°F. You should consider anything above 102.5° a fever.

Handling with "Kit" Gloves

Throughout this chapter you have learned all kinds of ways to keep your kitten healthy, from grooming to ear and eye cleaning. All these procedures have one thing in common. You have to be able to hold your kitten still.

I have found several different techniques helpful in handling squirming kittens: the scruff hold, the towel wrap, and the harness. I also list some useful tools. Just remember, the whole point of this section is to help you learn to gently hold your kitten so you can work on him without getting hurt yourself. You will be amazed at how quickly a cat can lash out, bite, or scratch you if he wants to get away—especially when water is involved.

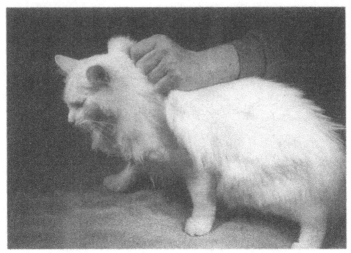

A scruff hold is when you grasp the fur between
the neck and shoulders, where the skin is loose.

Scruff Hold

The scruff of the neck is the nape of the neck where the skin is loose. Think of it as a built-in handle for kittens. The mother cat holds her kittens by the scruff when she moves them from one place to another, so kittens instinctively relax when held by the scruff. The scruff contains fewer nerve endings, so you won't cause your kitten pain by holding him there. Use your right hand if you're right-handed; your left if you're left-handed. Grab firmly, but gently. You're not trying to scare your kitten. The message you want to get across is that you are in control. A firm and steady hand tells your kitten, "Don't move until I release my grip."

The scruff hold is useful anytime you need your kitten to hold still. It's particularly useful for grooming, nail trimming, temperature taking, close examination, removing a tick, bathing, or anything that requires access to the body.

Towel Wrap

I have found that one of the best ways to keep all the sharp moving parts of your kitten in one place is to wrap him in a bath towel. There is a right way and a wrong way to do the towel wrap.

The towel must come up from underneath the neck so that the front paws are completely wrapped. Tuck one towel end into the side, then tuck other end under the kitten. This method of restraint is particularly helpful for working on the cat's head.

Cat Bag

Several commercially available cat bags can serve to restrain cats during bathing or administering medication. These bags come as either solid fabric,

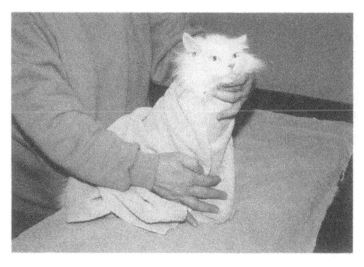

Another way to hold your kitten is to wrap him in a towel.

or a mesh to allow water to pass through. Think of a cat bag as a fancy towel wrap. Most of these bags are fitted for adult cats and aren't the right size for kittens. The trick to using the cat bag is getting the cat in the bag. Some uncooperative kittens are impossible to "bag." Therefore, I recommend the cat bag for very cooperative kittens for baths or giving medication.

Wearing Gloves Can Save Your Hands

No matter how good your kitten is, if you try to do something that annoys him, you can expect to get scratched. Wearing a pair of leather or canvas gloves can go a long way in protecting your hands. Gardening gloves can work, but leather gloves with a gauntlet to protect your wrists are better. Even though you loose some dexterity wearing a pair of heavy gloves, the protection from being mauled is well worth it. The person holding the cat usually wears the gloves while someone else works on the patient.

Making a Harness

During bathing, having your kitten in a sling or harness often helps. This gives you a handle and gives the kitten some range of freedom to move around without climbing out of the tub.

You can make a harness out of a dog leash or a piece of soft cotton rope, about three feet long. If you use a leash, make a loop and place one of the kitten's front legs through the loop. If you use a rope, make a slip knot in one end so that you form a loop. Then swing the end of the leash or rope around the other front leg so that it loops around the leg in a criss-cross fashion. You basically have made a figure eight with two loops around each front leg, and still

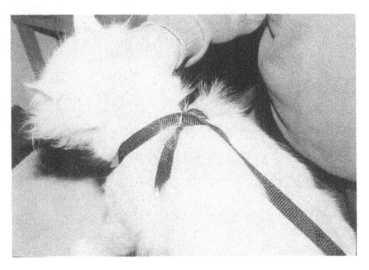

This instant-harness was made by wrapping a dog leash in loops around the front legs.

have a tail of the rope to hold on to. If you had to, you could actually use the harness to suspend the kitten off the floor without causing him any harm. This harness is particularly useful in the bath tub when the water starts spraying!

Kitten Taxi

How you transport your kitten home or to the first vet visit safely and in comfort can pose a special problem. The pet industry has designed an array of cat carriers, or *pet taxis*—basically boxes with air holes, a door or top lid, and a handle. They come in a variety of sizes, shapes and colors.

I've observed four basic types of carriers. First, the cardboard (although now they have plastic) boxes that open up on top that you get at the pet shops when you buy a kitten. They're cheap and meant to be used only once. If the kitten soils in the box, you can't clean it properly because the cardboard soaks up the mess. (The plastic ones can be washed and reused.)

Second, the carriers that airlines require for taking your kitten carry-on. These plastic boxes are squat and designed to fit under your seat. They have a metal grid for a top so that the kitten doesn't get completely claustrophobic. These carriers are too small for a large cat. Most kittens under six months old can fit for short periods of time.

Third, the larger carriers that are plastic, tall, have ample air vents all around, and have a large metal grid door in front that locks (these are the type of carrier I like to use). They come in all different sizes to accommodate all size cats. Some even have water and food dishes that clip onto the front door. They all have handles for easy carrying, and a few models even have wheels, like luggage.

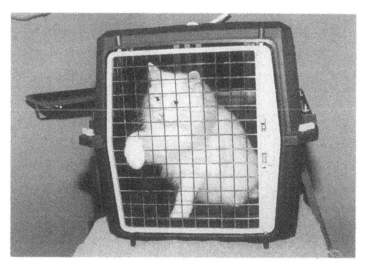

This kitten travels in an airline-type cat taxi.

Fourth, the newer soft duffle-like shoulder bags that are nylon with zippers. They have mesh panels at either end for air circulation and shoulder straps that make them light, airy, easy to carry, and durable. I also like these for travel in airports as carry-on luggage.

A Quick Guide to Which Restraint Is Best for the Job					
Job	**Scruff Hold**	**Towel Wrap**	**Cat Bag**	**Harness**	**Gloves**
Bathing			X	X	
Brush-out	X				X
Brushing Teeth		X	X		
Cleaning Ears		X	X		
Cleaning Eyes		X	X		
Dematting	X				X
Giving Ear Meds		X	X		
Giving Eye Meds		X	X		
Giving Oral Meds		X	X		
Taking Temp	X				X
Trimming Nails	X	X			X

Chapter 4

Feeding
and Nutrition

y now I'm sure you're all wondering what to feed your kitten. Just one
stroll down a pet aisle in the supermarket can confuse even the best
of shoppers. Don't despair, I'm going to give you a menu of your
kitten's dietary needs. As an appetizer, I provide some general background
information on nutrition and diet. For the salad, I furnish more specific
information on the nutritional needs of growing kittens. The main course
consists of the eating habits of kittens and cats, and dessert is a section on
dietary deficiencies and the harm they can do.

General Nutrition and Diet

The old saying, "You are what you eat," is
especially true of animals. All nutrients must
be in balance or nutritional deficiencies result.
Most kittens who eat a commercially prepared
diet eat a more balanced and complete diet
than we do, because extensive research has
gone into the daily requirements of animals.
Animal diets are closely regulated by the
National Research Council (NRC). When a commercial cat food claims to
be "complete and balanced," this means that it meets these daily
requirements. This standard has been set up by the AAFCO (Association of
American Feed Control Officials). As you can see, much thorough research
has gone into feeding our pets.

What Is a Nutrient?

Nutrients are substances required to sustain life. All diets consist of six main nutrients: water, protein, carbohydrates, fat, vitamins, and minerals. Table 4.1 gives more detail on each of them.

Let's look at each group a little more closely to give you an idea of why these nutrients are so important in the diet.

Water

Water is the single most important nutrient. Life can continue for weeks without nutrients in the food groups, but without water, clinical dehydration occurs within days. Severe dehydration of ten percent or more is terminal. Animals can get water naturally in two ways: by drinking and by consuming water via foods (this is very important for cats). Normal daily water intake for a cat is *one ounce per pound of body weight.* That's eight ounces of water, or one cup, for an average sized cat. Now if the cat climbs, frolicks, and chases mice, this amount can double. Dry kitten foods have about 10 percent moisture content, while canned foods have closer to 75 percent.

Most cats self-regulate their water. They sense their body dehydrating and seek water. Therefore, water should always be available. Several factors can increase water requirements and intake: heat, humidity, exercise, salty foods, and water loss from the body (fever, vomiting, and diarrhea).

Table 4.1   Nutrients and What They Do

Nutrient	Description
Water	Required daily to prevent dehydration and for normal bodily functions. Cats require less water than do dogs and humans.
Proteins	Building blocks of muscle, connective tissue, enzymes, and hormones. Cats require high levels of protein because they are carnivores.
Carbohydrates	Sources of energy, sugars, and fiber for normal digestion.
Fats	Essential for absorption of fat soluble vitamins, and provide storage for energy during lean times and fatty acids for the coat, as well as make food more palatable.
Vitamins	Necessary in small quantities for bodily functions.
Minerals	Required for strong bones, cellular function, and cell stability.

Protein

Proteins are the building blocks of muscle and connective tissues. Cats get their protein in their diet—usually animal source. Proteins are digested and broken down into *amino acids*, which are small molecules used for producing muscle fibers, hormones, and enzymes. There are 22 different amino acids. The kitten's liver can manufacture eleven of these, while the diet must account for eleven more. These 11 indispensable amino acids are called the *essential amino acids*.

We grade proteins as low or high quality. High quality proteins are ones which meet the following three requirements:

- They have high *biologic value*, which is a measure of the percent the body absorbs and utilizes. The body doesn't retain low quality proteins, it excretes them out in the urine.
- They contain all the *essential amino acids*.
- They have *digestibility*, which means that the body actually digests the protein, and doesn't just pass it out in the feces. A good digestibility is 80 percent in dry foods and 90 percent in canned. You can find good quality proteins with high digestibility in animal source foods, such as beef, lamb, poultry, and fish. Meat by-products and vegetable sources (such as soybean) aren't as good.

The quantity of protein also is crucial for kittens. The minimum protein level in a kitten's diet should be around 34 percent—10 percent higher than for adult cats. Before the body can utilize the maximum percent of protein from the food, however, it must take in a certain number of calories to use the protein. In other words, the diet might contain plenty of high-quality protein, but if it doesn't include a sufficient number of high-energy calories, the body can't use all the protein.

As mentioned, if the diet includes more protein than the kitten can use, the excess is excreted in the urine, which means the excess proteins must be filtered through the kidneys. All this filtering stresses the kidneys, and we believe it's a contributing factor in chronic kidney failure, a common ailment of older cats. We put these patients on a low-protein diet (usually less than 27 percent).

Carbohydrates

What would life be without carbs? This is the group of nutrients that includes *starches*, *sugars*, and *fiber*. Breads, pasta, cereal, rice, potatoes, vegetables, biscuits, cookies, and grains are all carbohydrates. Carbohydrates supply the majority of energy in a kitten's diet. If the diet includes too many carbohydrates, the body doesn't excrete them the way it does proteins. It stores them as energy, as fat. The body requires carbohydrates to utilize proteins. Too many carbohydrates, however, lead to obesity, a common problem in middle-aged cats.

There are three basic types of carbohydrates: *simple, complex,* and *dietary fiber.* Simple carbohydrates are the sugars. Complex carbohydrates are found in whole grains, fruits, vegetables. The foods composed of complex carbs are the ones that give sustained energy. Dietary fibers are the non-digestible carbohydrates, which aid in normal digestion. These fibers keep the food and stool moving through the intestines. Too many fiber-rich foods leads to diarrhea because they move through too quickly. Most kitten dry foods have about thirty percent total carbohydrates with three percent fiber.

Fats

Fats have received a lot of publicity lately, mostly bad. In people, diets high in fats have been linked to heart disease, obesity, and certain types of cancer. Saturated fats seem more culpable. Saturated fats are found in animal fats, hydrogenated vegetable oils, and tropical oils, such as palm seed and coconut oils. The unsaturated fats found in unprocessed vegetable oils seem to be the healthiest ones.

That said, let me now enumerate the good things fats and oils do. First, fats are needed in the diet to allow absorption of fat soluble vitamins (namely A, D, E, and K). Second, fats contain essential fatty acids essential for the synthesis of cell membranes and hormones, as well as for a healthy coat and skin. Deficiencies of fatty acids lead to skin and coat problems. Third, fats make foods *palatable,* meaning tasty. This is particularly true for cats. Either way, fats are a major part of their diets. Fourth, fats are easily digested and stored as a quickly mobilized energy source—body fat. Most kitten dry foods contain at least sixteen percent fat, whereas canned foods are closer to eight percent.

Vitamins

Do you take your vitamins? Most of the commercial kitten foods on the market are "complete and balanced," meaning, they contain the daily requirements for all nutrients, including vitamins and minerals. This implies that no supplements are necessary, and this generally is true. If you have a kitten who is extremely active or who has a special need or condition, its vitamin requirements will be higher. Before delving into what and how much to supplement, let's examine the vitamins your kitten needs.

There are two groups of vitamins: *water soluble* and *fat soluble.* Water soluble vitamins can dissolve in water, and are filtered through the kidneys when there is an excess of them in the body. Fat soluble vitamins are not dissolvable in water, and end up in places where fats congregate, such as the liver, skin, and blood. Table 4.2 lists the common vitamins and their functions.

Table 4.2 Common Vitamins and What They Do			
	Vitamin	**Natural Source**	**Functions**
Fat Soluble	A	orange vegetables	needed for sight, skin texture
	D	dairy foods	needed for strong bone, teeth, calcium, prevents Rickets
	E	oils and fats	antioxidant to maintain fats, muscle
	K	digestive by-products by-products	needed for blood clotting
Water Soluble	B1, B2, niacin, folic acid, biotin,	whole grains, eggs, oils	stimulates appetite, needed for normal cellular functions
	B6, B12 C	citrus fruits, vegetables	maintains immune system, prevents scurvy

Minerals

We collectively call minerals "ash." They are needed in minute quantities to sustain life. Minerals are fundamental building blocks of bone and teeth, and are required for various cellular functions. Minerals also are salts, which are crucial to maintaining tissues and cells. Some minerals are needed in fairly large amounts in the diet: calcium, iron, phosphorus, potassium, sodium, and zinc. Others are needed only in trace amounts, also from the diet: copper, iodine, magnesium, manganese, and selenium. Minerals basically come from foods, water, and salts. Table 4.3 shows the natural sources of some of these minerals.

Even though some of these minerals are required only in minute amounts, lacking them invites illness. Some specific mineral deficiencies are covered at the end of the chapter. Certain diseases stem from having too many of certain minerals in a cat's diet—mostly of the urinary tract. Chapter 20, "Urinary Diseases," furnishes the sordid details of these conditions.

Nutritional Needs of Growing Kittens

Kittens grow incredibly fast; sometimes several ounces a week. Kitten foods are formulated to be high in protein, fat, and energy. The quickest and easiest way to find out what amounts of nutrients are in a specific food is to read the "guaranteed analysis."

Table 4.3 Minerals: Their Source and Function

Mineral	Natural Source	Function
Calcium	bone meal	strong bones and teeth, cellular function
Copper	soybean	needed for blood cells, nerves, and bone
Iodine	seafood	needed for normal thyroid function
Iron	meats	oxygen transport of red blood cells
Magnesium	dairy foods, fish	needed for bone, muscle, heart function
Phosphorus	dairy foods	bone, teeth, kidney function
Potassium	dairy, fish, meats	nerves, heart rhythm, kidney function
Selenium	soybean	fat preservation, antioxidant
Sodium	meats	body water balance, all nerve function
Zinc	seafood, meats, eggs	healthy skin and coat

Guaranteed Analysis and Ingredients

How can you tell which foods are considered premium or "high quality"? Read the labels! Each package or can of cat food has a "guaranteed analysis" label. This is a measure of how much protein, fat, and water (moisture) is in the food, on a dry matter basis (discounting the water). They are rough estimates because they're listed as "not more than..." maximums for water and fiber, and "not less than..." minimums for protein and fat values. You've probably used this information from your food labels. I always check for grams of fat per ounce or serving, for example. Use the guidelines shown in Table 4.4 for an idea of what you can expect from a "premium" kitten food.

The other important thing to read on the food label is the list of ingredients. It lists all the ingredients in descending order of quantity—the first ingredient is what there is the most of, and the last one is in the least amount.

Table 4.4 Guidelines for Guaranteed Analysis in Premium Dry Kitten Foods *

Nutrient	Minimum %	Maximum %	Main Ingredient Source
Protein	34	N/A	chicken, seafood, lamb, beef
Fat	20	N/A	chicken fat, beef tallow, lamb fat, vegetable oil
Fiber	N/A	3	ground corn, rice, barley, bran, soybean
Water	N/A	10	N/A
Ash	N/A	7	bone meals

* these are averages
N/A = not applicable

Are All Cat Foods Alike?

The simple answer is "No." Most commercially available foods are "complete and balanced," but the similarity ends there. The differences lie in the quality of the ingredients, especially for protein. Here are some questions you should ask yourself before you buy kitten food:

- Should I buy a dry or canned food? Which one is better for my kitten?
- Is my kitten very active, or basically sedentary indoors?
- Will my kitten eat dry food, or have I already spoiled him with canned?
- Has my kitten shown an allergy to any main ingredient?
- Can I afford the expensive premium foods?
- Should I buy kitten food at a pet store, or grocery store?

It's time to take a closer look at the different types of kitten foods. On the surface, there are three forms of kitten food: dry, canned, and semimoist foods. Most veterinarians will recommend a dry food. These foods generally are more nutritious and better balanced by virtue of being mostly food and not water like the canned foods (canned foods are close to 75 percent water).

Also, as mentioned in Chapter 3, "Health Maintenance," dry foods are better for maintaining healthy teeth and gums than are canned foods. Canned foods are also more likely to put tartar on the teeth. I recommend keeping the canned food less than one-quarter of the daily intake by weight, if the owners insist on feeding it. Think of it as a treat, and not a main staple of the diet. As far as the semimoist foods go, I regard them as the "junk" foods, laden with salts, artificial colors, and preservatives.

The first way to classify cat foods is by the age group for which they're formulated: kitten, adult, or senior (less active). Since this is a kitten book, I focus on the kitten foods.

The second way to classify cat foods is by quality: premium and economy foods. These categories are based on the percentage of protein, fat, and fiber in the food, as well as the quality of the main ingredients, and whether they use preservatives or artificial ingredients. Generally speaking, the premium foods have higher levels of protein and fat and reduced mineral content. They also are more natural, with few if any artificial ingredients or preservatives added. *Remember:* Too much protein can stress the kidneys, but that's after years of consuming a high protein food. You don't need to worry about feeding a kitten too much protein. Table 4.5 summarizes what you can expect out of different types of foods.

Feeding Habits of Kittens

Cats have rather unique eating habits. Unlike us and dogs, cats are *free-choice feeders*, meaning they eat a little at a time, all day long. In other words, they "pick." Cats are born carnivores and naturally prefer high protein and fat diets. Domestic cats also happen to be very finicky eaters. Perhaps a better way to say it is that cats like variety in their diet. Anyone who has ever tried to feed a cat knows that the only thing that changes more than their taste is the weather. Just when you bought a whole case of their favorite food of the week, they take one sniff and walk away. Don't throw it away yet, by next week he'll be asking for it again. Let's face it, cats are finicky, fickle, fastidious, and fussy feeders.

What, How Much, and When To Feed

I tell my clients they should feed their kittens three to four times a day—a combination of kitten dry food and a teaspoon of canned mixed up together, and leave out a bowl of kitten dry food so they can come back and pick at their leisure. Always leave out a bowl of fresh water, especially if your kitten eats mostly dry food.

How much to feed is the next issue. Most bags and cans of kitten food have a guideline on the back label that lists feeding instructions. I have found that these guidelines often exaggerate the amount a kitten will eat in one day.

Table 4.6 gives you a basic idea of how much to feed your kitten for both dry and canned foods.

Your Overweight Kitten

Most people think that obesity is a problem of older cats. That's not always the case. Kittens reach adulthood between six and eight months of age, which is when most people spay and neuter them. At this point, your kitten is an adult for all practical purposes. Many people still feed kitten diets up to one year of age, however, which means that many kittens are being fed 20–30 percent more calories, and 6 percent more fat than they need. The kitten can end up obese by the time it's one year old. You might want to try leaving the food out for just a couple hours in the morning, then pick it up,

Table 4.5   Premium Kitten Food Analysis Comparison Chart *

Nutrient	Dry Food	Semimoist	Canned
Protein	34	24	12
Fat	20	8	8
Water	10	38	75
Fiber	3	3.5	1
Minerals (Ash)	7	5	2.5
Calories per ounce	100	80	30

* percentages for food "as fed" (out of package) are averages.

Table 4.6   Daily Amounts For Dry and Canned Kitten Foods

Age in Months	Cups per Day of Dry Food	Ounces of Canned Food
2	1/2 cup	6
3	1 cup	8
6-12	1 cup	10

Based on 8 oz. cups. Please use this chart as a guideline only. Watching weight gains and consulting with your vet are the best ways to determine if you're over- or underfeeding your kitten.

Hold the Milk

It seems like everyone for centuries has fed their kitten milk. I have no problem with this, as long as we're talking about young kittens under six months old. Up to that point, most kittens can still digest the sugar in milk, lactose. The problem is that a large percentage of kittens older than six months lose this ability to digest lactose, and become lactose intolerant. When your young adult kitten drinks milk, it causes stomach bloating and diarrhea. As a rule of thumb, hold the milk after six months of age.

---

instead of leaving it out all day long. You can then put it down again at dinner time for another couple of hours. This prevents her from "picking" on and off all day long.

Another cause of obesity is a sedentary lifestyle. Outdoor kittens who are always running, climbing, and jumping rarely get overweight, even if they're still on kitten food. You should take indoor cats off a kitten diet shortly after spaying or neutering to help guard against obesity. Other steps you might consider taking could be reducing the amount of food or increasing your kitten's exercise level.

Nutritional Deficiencies

Now that you know all the right things to feed your kitten, let's look at what can happen in the event of a deficiency of an individual nutrient. A lack of

This cat is *fat*—don't let your kitten develop a weight problem. *Carolyn Oderwald*

a nutrient leads to a nutritional deficiency and usually illness. Table 4.7 lists some of the commonly seen nutrient deficiencies and their symptoms.

Malnutrition

Let me say a word about general malnutrition. The first thing the body does when an animal ceases to take in food, such as in the case of starvation, is use readily available energy sources in the body. First, it draws from *glycogen* stores in muscle, which might last no more longer a few hours. After that, it absorbs fat and muscle tissue to provide energy. The only difference between starvation and malnutrition is that malnutrition isn't as extreme. Malnutrition involves a deficiency of one or more nutrients, whereas starvation involves deprivation of all nutrients.

Table 4.7   Nutritional Deficiencies

Nutrients	Deficiency Symptoms
Protein	dull brittle coat, low energy, muscle atrophy, swelling of legs
Carbohydrates/fiber	low energy, hypoglycemia, poor digestion, constipation
Fats/fatty acids	dry coat, flaky skin, dermatitis
Amino acid taurine	retinal degeneration, blindness, cardiomyopathy
Water	dehydration, dry gums, weight loss
Vitamins	
A	poor skin, dull coat, retinal degeneration, and blindness
B1,2,6,12	weight loss, poor appetite, poor digestion, convulsions, anemia, hind quarter weakness, and neck contortion
C	decreased immune system, scurvy
D	poor bone and teeth formation, rickets
E	poor muscle contractions, pansteatitis (inflammation of fat)
K	increased clotting time with excess bleeding, hemophilia

continues

Table 4.7 Nutritional Deficiencies
(continued)

Minerals	Deficiency Symptoms
Calcium	poor bone formation, skeletal deformities,
Iodine	hypothyroidism, goiter
Iron	anemia
Magnesium	bone and joint deformities, hyperextension of paws
Phosphorus	crazed appetite, poor bone formation, skeletal deformities
Potassium	neurological weakness, heart arrhythmia
Selenium	muscle degeneration
Sodium	excess urinations, dehydration, salt craving
Zinc	seborrhea, poor flaky coat, baldness

The best way to guard against nutritional deficiencies is to feed your kitten a premium commercial diet. I discourage homemade diets, even if you try to supplement it with vitamins and minerals. It still leaves essential fatty acids, calories, fiber, and other nutrients to balance. Even for a certified nutritionist, that's a tall order to fill. Take my advice and don't even try.

One last caution: Never, never feed your kitten raw meat. I know some books suggest it because it's supposedly "natural" for cats, but they mean wild cats. Domestic felines don't need raw meat in their diet. In fact, they can get serious diseases from undercooked meat and fish, such as internal parasites and toxoplasmosis.

Chapter 5

First Aid and
Household Hazards

This chapter could very well be the most important chapter in this book. Even if you didn't feed your kitten the best food or get all the vaccines on time, you wouldn't be immediately risking his life. But if you don't properly kitten-proof your home, you could be. Of all the chapters, this one requires the most interaction on your part. You need to make your house and yard safe for your kitten, as well as learn what household substances and people drugs could be deadly.

I also cover first aid for the most common home emergencies and tell you what to put in a first aid kit.

First Aid For Common Home Emergencies

First aid means just what it says—the *first* steps you take to *aid* in an emergency. The common emergencies covered in this chapter are burns, frostbite, bleeding, lamp cord shock, heat stroke, choking, bug bites, snake bites, fractures, shock and CPR, and poisonings. These aren't all of the possible disasters that can lurk in an average home, but they're the most common.

The most important thing to remember in an emergency is to *keep calm and level-headed.* Panicking doesn't help anyone. Keep your wits about you and try to remember what this chapter teaches you. I recommend that you read this chapter through to give you an idea of what to do in an emergency.

Also, this chapter is designed for use as a guide only. Always call your veterinarian in an emergency. Some people also call human health services, but these facilities might not be qualified to answer animal health related questions.

Burns

We have all been burned sometime or another—perhaps by a hot pot handle, candle, or stove. Kittens also get burned, from hot objects (called *thermal burns*) like the stove, or chemical burns from caustic substances around the house.

Burns come in different severity levels. Superficial burns (also called *first degree*) are minor burns that don't cause any damage beyond the first layers of the skin. These aren't serious and require little more than applying cold water or ice to the area to reduce the redness and swelling. Deep wounds are more serious because they cause damage to the deeper layers of the skin, causing blistering, destruction of the skin, loss of hair follicles, and scaring. These require immediate veterinary care.

The best thing you can do immediately is apply a clean, cool, damp towel to the burn, then cover the area with a clean or sterile bandage to control the bleeding and keep bacteria off. Your veterinarian has new methods of treating deep wounds, like antibiotics and new synthetic skin dressings that allow oxygen to get to the wound but still keep bacterial out. This speeds healing and lessens pain.

Chemical burns are treated differently. Acids or alkyl chemicals can burn skin similarly to heat except that the burn continues until the chemical is removed from the skin. Immediately read the label and see if it says how to treat skin contact. Follow the directions. If you have any questions, call your veterinarian. Use copious amounts of water to flush the area. Be careful not to get the chemical on you. Wear gloves and protect your eyes. Your kitten could be frantic, so consult the "Handle with Kit Gloves" section at the end of Chapter 3, "Health Maintenance," to restrain him safely. Seek professional help as soon as you can.

Frostbite

Frostbite is an unfortunate condition that occurs when tissues are subjected to extreme cold for prolonged periods. The most common sites affected are the tips of the ears, toes, and tail. It occurs when the skin actually freezes. I most often see frostbite in outdoor cats during January and February. Frozen skin doesn't stay viable, turns bright red, then black, and finally dies. During the initial freezing there is pain. After the tissue devitalizes, feeling in it ceases. Most cases of frostbite require some measure of surgical correction.

The best thing you can do is keep your kitten indoors when the temperature falls below freezing. If he gets out, slowly warm his extremities. Never rub or pour hot water on the skin. Use warm compresses to slowly warm up the ears and tail. Seek professional help.

Bleeding

Most bleeding comes from cuts and scrapes. Since kittens get into everything, don't be surprised if he accidentally cuts or scrapes himself. Most minor cuts or abrasions only bleed slowly, which means the wound only oozes venous blood. If an artery is severed, the bleeding is profuse and spurting. Follow the directions below to stop the bleeding:

- **Venous oozing.**   Usually all you need to do is apply direct pressure to the site, using a clean pad or folded cloth for five minutes. If that doesn't work, elevate the body part and apply pressure with ice. Seek professional advice for follow-up care.

- **Arterial bleeding.**   Act quickly. Blood will be spurting out from the cut. Immediately apply firm, even pressure over the cut. Elevate the body part and use an ice pack. Apply the pressure for five minutes. Sometimes, you will need to use a tourniquet. You can make one out of a rope, a strip of cloth, or belt. The principle is to tie the tourniquet about the wound and tighten sufficiently to stop or slow down the bleeding. Never leave a tourniquet on for more than ten minutes— doing so can cause irreparable damage to the tissues. If getting your animal to the clinic takes longer than ten minutes, you'll have to loosen it for a minute every ten minutes to allow blood flow to the area. Of course, never use the tourniquet around the head or neck. You will need prompt veterinary attention, so don't delay.

Regardless of the type of bleeding, most cuts and lacerations require professional veterinary care. I treat wounds four ways:

1. Stop the bleeding
2. Clean the wound and apply antibiotic ointment
3. Suture deep lacerations if stitches are necessary
4. Apply a sterile bandage

Lamp Cord Shock

Kittens love to chew on dangling things. All those electric lamp cords hanging around the house are perfect playthings in a kitten's mind. What happens if she bites through to the electric wire? At the very least, an electrical burn occurs in the mouth and on the tongue. This blistering and blackening is very painful and can get infected. Even this requires prompt veterinary care. Most veterinarians treat oral electrical burns with antibiotics and anti-inflammatory drugs for the blistering and pain.

Severe cases of electric lamp cord shock—electrocution, cardiac arrest, and fluid in the lungs—can lead to sudden death. This requires immediate cardiopulmonary resuscitation (CPR) attempts. A section on CPR follows later in this chapter.

Heat Stroke

Heat stroke also is known as *heat prostration*. It occurs when a kitten is kept in a hot environment for too long. The most common place is a closed car during warm weather. *Never leave your kitten in a closed car if the ambient temperature is higher than 68°F.* In such a situation, the internal car temperature can approach 120°F. Since cats cannot sweat, but rely on panting to cool themselves, their internal body temperature rises quickly. A rectal temperature exceeding 105°F can be life-threatening.

Symptoms of heat stroke could be panting, beet-red mucous membranes, weakness, vomiting, bleeding from body orifices, seizure, and ultimately death. Treatment needs to commence immediately. You must slowly but steadily bring the kitten's body temperature down to below 103°F. Wrap him in wet, cold towels; and pouring cool, not cold, water over the body, concentrating on the abdomen and paws. While you do cool him down, quickly get him to your veterinarian. There, the vet can give your kitten intravenous fluids to correct dehydration and blood tests to check for evidence of internal organ system damage.

Choking

The first thing you'll notice if your kitten's got something stuck in her mouth or throat is coughing and gasping sounds—like a cough. The tissues of the mouth might appear blue. Kittens get very frantic when they're scared. Wrap him in a towel, and have someone else help hold him while you open his mouth. Look for any objects caught in the throat. Use a flashlight for good lighting. If you see the object, try grasping it with your fingers or tweezers. If you cannot see the object, or cannot grab it, then you should use the *Heimlich maneuver* to try to dislodge it.

To perform the Heimlich maneuver, lay the kitten down on his side or hold him upright. Cup your strong hand around the chest, just behind the ribcage. Squeeze forcibly, but be careful not to crush the ribs. This pushes air out of the lungs and hopefully dislodges the obstruction. You might have to do this several times. If possible, you should be doing the Heimlich manuever on the way to the veterinary hospital to maximize time. If your attempts are unsuccessful, your veterinarian will have to perform a *tracheotomy* (puncturing of the wind pipe)to allow breathing.

Bug Bites

Several bugs have stinging or poisonous bites. Others are just annoying. Stinging bugs are bees and spiders. Ticks bite and attach, but do not sting. This section covers each.

Bee Stings

The most common bees are wasps, hornets, yellow jackets, bumble bees, and honey bees. Some are more aggressive than others, with hornets and yellow jackets topping the list. All bees have a stinging bite that burns and causes an immediate localized inflammation. Most stung kittens try to run away from the pain, so you might see them running in circles crying out.

If your kitten stumbles on a bee nest, try to whisk him away without getting stung yourself. Immediately put ice on the bite to reduce pain and swelling. Use a magnifying glass to look for a stinger. Some bees leave their stinger in the skin. Use rubbing alcohol or hydrogen peroxide to disinfect the bite and a pair of tweezers to pull out the stinger. Apply an antibacterial ointment on the bite after you finish treating it.

The most important thing to watch for immediately following a bee sting is an allergic reaction—*bee sting allergy*. Rarely, but often enough to watch out for, do kittens have a severe allergic reaction (called *anaphylaxis*, or *histamine shock*) to a bee sting. When they do, the entire body goes into shock, and breathing becomes difficult, then impossible, as the tissues of the throat swell to the point of closing over. The kitten's life is immediately in jeopardy.

The best thing you can do is get your kitten to a veterinarian immediately, who will give him a shot of *adrenaline*, the antidote to anaphylaxis. If you know your kitten is allergic to bee stings, you might want to ask your veterinarian for a pre-measured shot of adrenaline to have on hand in case of emergency. Of course, you would need to be trained to administer the shot properly. If that isn't recommended, then you could use over-the-counter antihistamines, such as Benadryl, as a second choice. Ask your vet what would be the appropriate dose for your kitten.

Spider Bites

The spiders that have toxic bites are the Brown's spider and the Black Widow. The same information as bee stings apply for spider bites, except you don't need to bother trying to find stingers. Also, fewer kittens are allergic to spider bites. Even though anaphylaxis is not a concern, local swelling and pain are common. The treatment for spider bites is the same as for bee stings.

Tick Bites

Ticks don't sting or cause anaphylaxis, but they sure can be annoying. Ticks are blood-sucking insects that carry diseases like Lyme disease, Rocky Mountain Spotted Fever (RMSF), Ehrlichiosis, and Babesiosis. Luckily, cats are fairly resistant to Lyme disease and RMSF. The tick attaches to the skin by its mouth parts, which are like small barbed fish hooks. You often can see a local reaction at the bite site owing to a mild allergy to the tick's saliva. This manifests as pain, swelling, redness, and possibly infection of the skin.

Once embedded, a tick is difficult to remove. The best way I know for removing ticks is to first stun them with rubbing alcohol. Wet a cotton ball with rubbing alcohol and apply it to the tick for 30 seconds. Then use a fine, pointed tweezers to grasp the bug right where it attaches to the skin. Give a quick pull straight out. You might hear a click. The body of the tick should be in your tweezers. Occasionally the head of the tick snaps off and remains buried in the skin, because it's barbed like a fish hook. Vets don't usually dig these heads out, and despite old wives tales, they do not regrow a new tick. Disinfect the bite with hydrogen peroxide and apply an antibiotic skin ointment to prevent infection.

Snake Bites

In certain parts of the country, snake bites are a real threat to an inquisitive, curious kitten. Snakes come in two varieties: venomous (meaning poisonous) and nonvenomous (not poisonous). When a nonvenomous snake bites an animal, it can leave a nasty wound, but you don't have to worry about any toxins. Veterinarians usually clean out the wound and put the kitten on antibiotics. When a venomous snake bites your kitten, on the other hand, you have to act immediately to save his life.

North America has several poisonous snakes species, all of which belong to the *Pit Viper* family. You can recognize them by their two long fang teeth and a pit, or hole, between their eyes and nostrils. The most common species are cobra, copperhead, coral snake, cottonmouth, diamondback rattlesnake, and water moccasin.

The symptoms of a snake bite are dramatic—explosive swelling and bruising around the bite punctures, swelling of the face, and breathing difficulties—and can progress to seizures, coma, and death within hours. Timing is crucial for survival. Here are a few first aid steps you can take to better your kitten's chances of survival:

First Aid for Snake Bites

- Keep your kitten calm, even if that means wrapping him in a towel and holding him tightly.

- Tie a string or shredded piece of cloth to act as a tourniquet above the bite (if it's on a limb but not if it's on the face) to slow down the spread of the venom. Loosen the homemade tourniquet for one minute every ten minutes to avoid damaging the limb.

- Flush out the bite holes with warm water or hydrogen peroxide. I don't recommend "sucking out the venom with your mouth" as was once taught in first aid manuals. There are suction pumps available in If you happen to have a human first aid kit, it should contain a suction pump, which you can use instead of sucking.

- Get your kitten to a veterinary facility ASAP, where a vet can begin intravenous fluids, antivenom injections, and treatment for shock.

Fractures

Kittens love to jump. They're always jumping on and off of things—sofa to window sill, countertop to refrigerator. Not to mention climbing trees and jumping over fences. The first thing you would notice if your kitten fractured a bone is holding up the injured leg and limping on three legs. We call this being "three-legged lame." *If you attempt to touch the leg, you will likely get a reaction, so be careful.* Cats in pain are likely to lash out, even at their favorite people.

Fractures are either *simple* or *complicated* (or *compound*). Simple fractures are where the broken ends of the bone stay under the skin. Complicated fractures are where one or both of the broken ends of the bone protrude through the skin. This latter scenario is worse because it allows bacteria to contaminate the fracture, possibly setting up infection. Chapter 19, "Orthopedic Problems," offers a complete description of fractures.

You should immobilize and cover your kitten's fracture before you take him to the vet. Perform the following instructions.

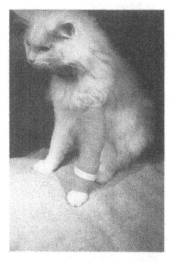

To stabilize a fracture, place a straight, long rod by the limb, then wrap strips of clean cloth around the leg and splint material.

Preparing a Fractured Leg for Transport

Make a homemade splint to immobilize the fractured leg. Find a straight rod about six to ten inches long, such as a pencil. Before your splint can effectively immobilize the fracture site, it must be long enough to span between the joint above and below the fracture. If the fracture were of the forearm, for example, the splint would need to immobilize from the elbow to the wrist. Place the splint along the leg, then wrap strips of clean cloth around both the leg and splint material so that when you're done, the leg cannot bend and any wound is covered.

Cat Fight Wounds and Abscesses

Most wounds resulting from cat fights are either scrapes and cuts, or bites. If you know of rabies in your area, don't handle the wounds with bare hands—wear gloves. Wrap your kitten in a towel so you don't get scratched. I like using hydrogen peroxide to wash out the wounds because it's an excellent antiseptic. Let the peroxide "fizz" for a minute, then pat dry and apply a triple antibiotic ointment to the wound.

Minor scratches and cuts don't necessarily require veterinary attention. Punctures and bites *always* do, because bites have a tendency in cats to *abscess*. An abscess is a pocket of infection and pus trapped below the skin. What happens is that the puncture brings bacteria from the mouth or nails of the attacking cat down below the skin of your kitten. The skin heals over quickly, often within a day or so, but the bacteria festers underneath, forming an

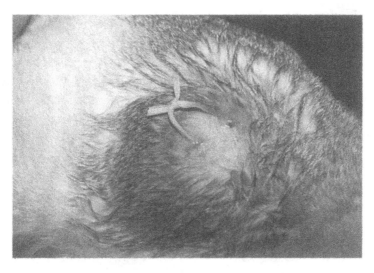

A typical cat abscess with a drain in it.

abscess. The abscess manifests as a swelling and is very painful to your kitten. You might notice the scabbed puncture wound at the center of the swelling.

Other symptoms are fever, loss of appetite and lethargy. Abscesses generally take three days to form. The treatment is to lance the abscess and drain the infection, then flush out the wound and place the kitten on antibiotics. The kitten usually need to be under a general anesthetic or heavy sedation during this procedure.

Cat fights are cause for additional concern, as well. Certain feline viruses can spread from one cat to another through bites: feline leukemia, feline immunodeficiency virus, and feline infectious peritonitis, all three of which are discussed in Chapter 2, "First Visit to the Veterinarian's." I recommend to all my clients to vaccinate their kittens for as many of these diseases as they can before letting them go outside.

Shock

Shock is a life-threatening condition that occurs when blood pressure falls dramatically and suddenly. Several conditions can cause shock, including sudden blood loss, poisonings, and severe trauma or fright.

Whether your kitten survives depends on how quickly you can respond. He might be semi-conscious or unconscious. The symptoms of shock are as follows:

- Low blood pressure
- Increased heart rates of over 200 beats per minute
- Rapid shallow breathing
- Unconsciousness or disorientation
- Fixed dilated pupils
- Collapse, fainting, or coma

A veterinarian treats shock very aggressively with intravenous fluids, drugs to increase the blood pressure. If bleeding is the cause, it must be stopped first. Table 5.1 outlines some common methods and drugs for treating shock. You can do some of these, while a veterinarian must do the others.

Cardiopulmonary Resuscitation (CPR)

This is one of those things you hope you never need to know, but which you absolutely should know nevertheless. CPR is required when the heart and breathing stop, causing a sudden drop in blood pressure, called *cardiac arrest*.

CPR consists of three components: establish an airway, breathe for the animal, and cardiac assistance, known as the ABC's of CPR. The following list describes each component so you'll know how to perform them in an emergency.

Perform mouth-to-muzzle resuscitation by forming a passageway of air from your mouth to the kitten's nose with your hand. Breathe gently and regularly.

1. **Airway.** The very first thing you must do is make sure nothing is blocking the airway. Keep it open by stretching out the head and neck and pulling out the tongue.

2. **Breathing.** You must breathe for your kitten. The best way to do so is mouth-to-muzzle breathing. Hold your hand over your kitten's nose and mouth. Cup your hand so you can breathe into your hand so that the air goes up his nose. Do this gently or you can damage his lungs. You should only breathe hard enough to get a slight rise in his chest wall. Repeat this every 30 seconds. You are now breathing for him.

3. **Cardiac.** You must pump the blood for your kitten since his heart has stopped. You must do this by laying your kitten on his side. Cup his chest in your stronger hand so that if you try to squeeze your fingers and thumb together your hand is right behind his elbows. Press hard enough to compress his chest, but not hard enough to crack the ribs. Do this every five seconds.

I know this all sounds difficult. It's preferable to have two people for CPR—one doing the breathing, the other doing the chest compression. If you're alone, do the best you can. You must alternate between the two. During all this, try to assess your progress:

- Does he start breathing on his own?
- Does a pink color return to his gums?

- Do you start to feel a heart beat?
- Does consciousness return?

Do the best you can; remember, you're trying to perform a miracle.

Table 5.1 Shock Therapy	
Treatment or Procedure	**Effect on System**
IV fluids*	Increase blood volume to better perfusion of organ systems
Open airway	Ensures that there is no obstruction to breathing
Stop all bleeding	Hemorrhage control measures for arterial and venous hemorrhage
Keep in laying position with head downward	Keeps the blood flow directed to the head and brain, where it's most crucial
Keep warm with heating pads and blankets	During shock, body temperature usually falls causing hypothermia (to temperatures below 99°F)
Blood transfusions*	Corrects blood loss of greater than 30 percent
Check for heart rate quality of pulse	Heart rate usually increases during and shock (approximately 150–250 beats per minute) and the pulses get weak and "thready"
Check mucus membrane color and capillary refill time	The mucus membranes of the mouth become white in shock, and when you press on gums, it takes more than two seconds for the color to come back
Monitor for urine output, if none, increase IV fluids increasing diuretic drugs*	When the blood perfusion to the kidneys is low, urine production stops; the amount of fluids given intravenously and using diuretic drugs that increase urine production, reverses this condition
Injections of Cortisone*	Stabilizes blood vessels, increases oxygenation of the blood, and increases blood flow
Perform CPR	Returns blood pressure and oxygenation of tissues

* Denotes treatments and procedures a veterinarian must perform

Household Poisons

Many hidden poisons lie in wait in the average household, and because kittens have an uncanny way of getting into places they shouldn't—places where poisonous household substances are stored—knowing what's what is especially important. The good news is that most kittens are discriminating eaters and don't put just anything in their mouth like babies or puppies.

Most hazardous products have warnings on their label. They could cause skin or eye irritation, stomach irritation, or be toxic. If you're not sure whether a given substance is toxic, call your local poison control center.

Table 5.2 lists most of the common toxic household substances, including symptoms and the basic first aid.

Table 5.2   Common Household Toxic Substances

Substance	Symptoms	Basic First Aid
Acetone	Vomiting diarrhea, depression, weak pulse pulse, shock	Induce vomiting[1], give baking soda in water orally
Ammonia	Vomiting blood, abdominal pain, skin blisters and burns	Wash skin with water and vinegar, give dilute water and vinegar orally or three egg whites
Antifreeze	Vomiting, coma, kidney failure, death	Induce vomiting[1], administer 1 oz. of vodka orally followed by water, can be repeated
Aspirin	Vomiting, excess bleeding, acid odor to breath	Induce vomiting[1], give baking soda mixed in water orally to counteract acid overdose
Bleach	Burns to skin and mouth, vomiting	Induce vomiting[1], give three egg whites
Carbon monoxide	Dullness, depression, dilated pupils after being in a garage with a car	Mouth-to-muzzle resuscitation[2], get to fresh air immediately
Charcoal Lighter	Vomiting, breathing distress, shock, coma or seizures	Induce vomiting[1], give laxatives[2]
Chocolate, milk and dark varieties	Vomiting, diarrhea, depression, heart arrhythmia, muscle twitching, seizures, coma from high levels of caffeine and theobromine	Induce vomiting[1], give laxatives[2] Lethal doses of ⅛ oz. per lb. for dark chocolate, and 1 oz. per pound for milk chocolate

continues

Common Household Toxic Substances

Substance	Symptoms	Basic First Aid
Deodorants	Vomiting	Induce vomiting[1]
Detergents/soap	Vomiting	Induce vomiting[1], give laxatives[2], give three egg whites or milk orally, watch breathing
Furniture polish	Vomiting, breathing distress, shock, coma, or seizures	Induce vomiting[1], give laxatives[2]
Gasoline	Skin irritation, weakness, dementia, dilated pupils vomiting, twitching	Induce vomiting[1], give laxatives[2], vegetable oil orally to block absorption, get into fresh air
Kerosene/Fuel Oil	Vomiting, breathing distress, shock, coma, or seizures	Induce vomiting[1], give laxatives[2], give vegetable oil orally to block absorption
Lead	Vomiting, diarrhea, anemia, neurologic symptoms, blindness, seizures, coma	Induce vomiting[1], give laxatives[2], remove source of lead—paint chips,car battery, leaded gasoline, plumbing solder, grease, pellets, fishing anchors, golf balls, shotgun shot
Lime	Skin irritant, burns	Wash skin with copious soap and water
Lye	Vomiting blood, abdominal pain, skin blisters and burns	Wash skin with water and vinegar, give dilute water and vinegar orally or three egg whites
Organophosphate insecticides	Excess drooling, weakness, seizures, vomiting, dilated pupils	Wash off insecticide, administer atropine sulfate as the antidote
Paint thinner	Vomiting, breathing distress, shock, coma,or seizures	Induce vomiting[1], give laxatives[2]
Phenol cleaners	Nausea, vomiting, shock, liver or kidney failure	Wash off skin, induce vomiting[1], give three egg whites or milk orally
Rat poison	Excess bleeding, anemia, cyanosis	Induce vomiting[1], requires vitamin K injections

continues

Common Household Toxic Substances		
Substance	**Symptoms**	**Basic First Aid**
Rubbing alcohol	Weakness, incoordination, blindness, coma, dilated pupils, coma, vomiting, and diarrhea	Induce vomiting[1], give baking soda in water to neutralize acidosis
Strychnine	dilated pupils, respiratory distress, rigid muscles, seizures, and spasms with loud noises or stimulus, brown urine	Induce vomiting[1], keep kitten in a dark quiet room until can transport to a veterinary facility
Turpentine	Vomiting, diarrhea, bloody urine, neurologic disorientation, coma, breathing distress	Induce vomiting[1], give vegetable oil by mouth to block absorption, give laxatives
Tylenol®	Depression, fast heart rate brown, urine, anemia	Induce vomiting[1], give 500mg of vitamin C per 25 lb., followed by baking soda in water

[1]Induce vomiting by giving one teaspoon of hydrogen peroxide orally. Repeat as needed to stimulate vomiting. Another way to induce vomiting is by giving ½ teaspoon of the emetic, Ipecac Syrup® (Paddock Laboratories, Minneapolis, MN, 55427), available in all pharmacies and a valuable agent for stimulating vomiting.
[2]Laxatives serve to quickly expel the plant material from the intestines. Mineral oil is a safe and effective laxative. Give ½ teaspoon. It doesn't work immediately, but you usually see the offending material pass through in the stool within 24 hours.
*Described earlier in this chapter.

Poisonous Plants

You might be asking yourself, "Why should I be concerned about poisonous plants—it's not like cats eat plants..." Wrong. Kittens love to nibble on plants—even dried flowers. To satisfy this grazing urge, you can buy cat grass from the pet stores, which you can grow and let your little darling nibble on. Don't ever let him chew on indoor or garden plants because many of them are poisonous to cats. The consequences can range from an upset stomach to death. You should go over tables 5.3 and 5.4 and see how many you have in your home or yard.

Table 5.3 Poisonous Household Plants

Plant Common Name	Symptoms
Cactus	Needle injury, scratched eyes, needle in tongue
Dumb Cane (Dieffenbachia)	Numbing of mouth, blistering in mouth, excess salivation, swollen tongue
Marijuana	Hallucinations
Mistletoe*	Vomiting and diarrhea, slowed pulse
Philodendron	Mouth burns and blistering, throat irritation, excess salivation, swollen tongue
Poinsettia Sap	Vomiting and diarrhea
Tobacco	Vomiting, nausea, excess salivation, increased heart rate

*Denotes a potentially lethal plant toxicity

Table 5.4 Poisonous Outdoor and Garden Plants

Plant Common Name	Symptoms
Acorns	Kidney failure
Apple seed	Vomiting, trouble breathing, coma
Azalea bush swallowing	Excess salivation, vomiting, excess
Bird of Paradise flower	Vomiting, diarrhea, abdominal pain, and cramps
Castor bean*	Abdominal pain, shock, low blood pressure
Cherry tree seeds	Vomiting, trouble breathing, coma
Daffodil flower bulb	Nausea, vomiting
English holly	Vomiting, diarrhea, abdominal pain and cramps

continues

Table 5.4 Poisonous Outdoor and Garden Plants (continued)

Plant Common Name	Symptoms
English Ivy berries	Vomiting, diarrhea, abdominal pain and cramps
Honeysuckle	Vomiting, diarrhea, abdominal pain and cramps
Horse chestnut	Vomiting, diarrhea, abdominal pain and cramps
Iris flower bulb	Vomiting, diarrhea, abdominal pain and cramps
Lily of the Valley	Vomiting, diarrhea, heart arrhythmia
Morning Glory flower	Hallucinations
Nutmeg	Hallucinations
Oleander*	Vomiting, diarrhea, heart arrhythmia
Potato Skins with green buds	Dry mouth, vomiting, diarrhea
Rhododendron shrub	Excess salivation, vomiting, excess swallowing
Rhubarb	Vomiting, diarrhea, depression
Skunk Cabbage	Burning of mouth and tongue, excess salivation, swollen throat
Tulip Flower Bulb	Vomiting, diarrhea, abdominal pain and cramps
Wild mushroom*	Central nervous system disturbances, coma
Wisteria flower	Nausea, vomiting
Yew shrub berries*	Vomiting, diarrhea, wide pupils, heart arrhythmia, convulsions

*Denotes a potentially lethal plant toxicity

The dumb cane (left) and poinsettia (right)
plants are both harmful to kittens if ingested.

First Aid Considerations in Plant Poisoning

Regardless of the type of plant poisoning, you can do a few first aid techniques in case of accidental ingestion of a poisonous plant. These first aid measures in no way replace prompt veterinary care. These are the steps you should take immediately if you notice the plant being eaten.

1. Identify the plant. Knowing ahead of time what plants you have inside your house and in your yard is a good idea. Don't wait for an emergency, then start frantically trying to identify the plant.

2. Try to figure out how recently your kitten ingested the plant. Get a rough idea—was it minutes or hours ago? How much of the plant is left? Try to visualize how much of it the kitten consumed—was it just one leaf or half the plant?

3. Call your veterinarian poison control center for advice. They will ask you what plant, how long ago, and how much of it the kitten ate. If you can't reach anyone, go on to step 4.

4. The single most important way to treat plant poisonings is to remove the source of the toxin, which usually means getting the plant out of his digestive tract.

You can remove a plant from a kitten's digestive tract in one of two ways if the plant was just consumed minutes ago:

- Induce vomiting by giving one teaspoon of hydrogen peroxide orally. Repeat as needed to stimulate vomiting.

- Administer one-half teaspoon of the emetic, Ipecac® syrup. This is available in all pharmacies and is a valuable agent for stimulating vomiting. Repeat as needed.

If the plant was consumed more than an hour ago, get professional help. These cases are beyond simple first aid. Call your vet! A veterinarian can do a number of other things, depending on the type of plant, and the severity of the poisoning, some of which are mentioned in the following list:

- Administer IV fluids as supportive care
- Perform stomach pumping
- Give activated charcoal to absorb the plant toxins
- Give an enema to help expel the plant material from the bowel
- Treat secondary symptoms of certain plant poisonings, like heart arrhythmia, seizure, dehydration, and respiratory distress.

Remember, don't panic, most kittens don't usually eat enough of a plant to cause a life-threatening situation, but to be sure, call your veterinarian.

First Aid Kit for Kittens

Everyone who has a kitten needs to assemble a first aid kit in case of emergencies. Believe me, you do need it from time to time. You should include certain basics in the kit to treat most emergency situations, or at least until you can transport her to the animal hospital. Always keep the kit handy, and take it with you when you travel with your kitten.

- Ace bandage
- Antibiotic skin ointment

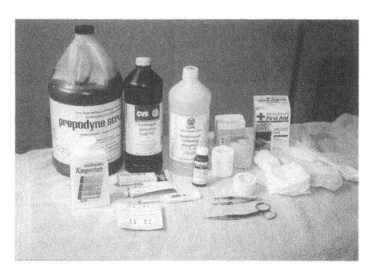

Supplies for your kitten's first aid kit.

- Antihistamine tablets
- Bandage scissors
- Gauze, 2-inch rolls and 2-inch 3 2-inch squares
- Hydrocortisone skin ointment
- Hydrogen peroxide
- Ipecac syrup
- Kaopectate
- Latex exam gloves
- Medical tape (white) 1-inch roll
- Nonstick pads
- Pediatric electrolyte oral solution
- Petroleum jelly (white)
- Povidone antiseptic solution
- Rectal thermometer
- Rubbing alcohol
- Splinter tweezers

Chapter 6

Skin Diseases

The second part of this book is a collection of chapters, each of which covers a specific organ system of your kitten and the most common diseases that can affect that system. Use this part of the book as a reference guide. Look up the specific disease in which you're interested. The information is presented in an overview style. If you're looking for very detailed information regarding a specific disease, please consult your veterinarian.

This chapter covers the most common skin diseases of kittens. I try to give you a summary of each disease in a summary box, which includes the most common symptoms, the diagnostic test most commonly used, and some common treatment options. The box would look something like this:

Disease Info Box	
Disease	disease
Common Symptoms	symptoms
Diagnosis	diagnosis
Treatment Options	treatment

The info box is great for at-a-glance information on a specific disease, but you should read the text for more details.

Acne

Acne in cats very much resembles acne in adolescents. It involves blackheads and pustules (white heads) that are painful and can erupt a white pus-like material. In cats, acne occurs on the chin. It can start at the time of puberty, but it can occur at any age. Most people think their kitten has a "dirty" chin because the black heads leave a black residue.

Staphylococcus bacteria is often a bacteria that infects the hair follicles in acne. The chin can become very swollen. Most veterinarians can diagnose acne just by the way it looks. A bacterial culture could be necessary if it becomes severe. Treatment is difficult because the pustules often reoccur. Washing the chin with antibacterial soaps and applying an antibiotic ointment might be all you have to do. More severe cases require oral antibiotics.

Your kitten's "dirty" chin might actually be a case of feline acne.

Disease Info Box

Disease	Acne
Common Symptoms	Pustules on chin
Diagnosis	Clinical appearance
Treatment Options	Washing, topical or systemic antibiotics

Allergic (Miliary) Dermatitis

This skin disease is very common in cats who have skin allergies. Miliary means "many bumps," and that's exactly what these kittens feel like. Many small bumps and scabs cover certain areas of the body, especially the abdomen and lower back. The bumps are actually excoriations capped with crust. Think of them as like hives in people. Miliary dermatitis has several different causes all involving immune type, or allergic reactions:

- Drug reactions
- Flea bites
- Food allergies
- Inhalant allergies
- Mange mite bites
- Nutritional deficiency
- Staphylococcus skin infections

If you notice many bumps and scabs on your kitten's
skin, as shown, he might have miliary dermatitis.

Most people notice the bumps when they run their hand along the
kitten's back. Your veterinarian checks for all the above external parasites, as
well as for allergies. Testing for allergies has gotten very sophisticated. Your
veterinarian should be able to run three screens:

- **Inhalant allergies.** Things your kitten inhales, such as pollen, mold
  spores, trees, grasses, and weeds
- **Indoor allergies.** Things found inside the house, such as household
  dust, cigarette smoke, and molds
- **Food allergies.** Meats, soybean, cornmeal, fillers, dairy, and seafood

The vet performs these tests as a blood RAST (Radioallergosorbent
Test), which measures the body's immune response, that is, antibodies, to
specific allergies. The test gives the veterinarian an idea of the things to
which your kitten is allergic. Some of these things can be simple to eliminate
from his environment, such as a wool rug or cigarette smoke. Other things,
like pollens and dust, aren't so easy. A food allergy forces you to find a food
that doesn't contain the ingredient to which the cat is allergic.

Treatment is twofold: treat the allergy that causes the skin eruption, and
give anti-inflammatory drugs to reduce the hives, itching, and hair loss. The
drug most commonly prescribed is *cortisone*, a powerful anti-inflammatory
that temporarily halts the allergic reaction. Human antihistamine drugs do
little good in cats. Treating the allergy is a bit more complicated. If you can't
limit the exposure of the allergy, then your veterinarian can have a serum
custom-made to your kitten's allergies, and give regular increasing injections
of them to desensitize your kitten. These are the same as *allergy shots* given to

people who are allergic to something, done slowly over months. You can see, it's a commitment in time and money.

Disease Info Box	
Disease	Allergic (miliary) dermatitis
Common Symptoms	Itching, hair loss, bumps and scabs
Diagnosis	Allergy testing, checking for parasites
Treatment Options	Insect control, cortisone drugs, allergy shots

Alopecia (Hair Loss)

Alopecia just means hair loss, or baldness. Many things can cause hair loss, including some of the more common:

- **Allergic dermatitis.**   Allergies to food, fleas, and indoor or outdoor substances
- **Overgrooming.**   Cats who literally lick themselves bald
- **External parasites.**   Fleas, ticks, mange, and lice
- **Hormonal changes.**   Affects primarily females during heat and post queening, symmetrical over trunk and under abdomen
- **Inherited baldness.**   Usually seen in Siamese-type cats on ear tips and temples and Sphynx cats. The Sphynx breed is born bald
- **Nutrition.**   Nutritional deficiencies can cause hair loss
- **Ringworm fungus.**   Crusting and patchy hair loss from fungal infection
- **Skin infection.**   Bacterial infections of the hair follicle can lead to hair loss
- **Shedding to an extreme.**   Seasonal for outdoor cats, all year round for indoor in warm climates

Disease Info Box	
Disease	Alopecia
Common Symptoms	Hair loss and baldness
Diagnosis	Skin bacterial and fungal cultures, skin scrapings, hormonal tests, allergy tests,
Treatment Options	Varied with cause

Cuterebra Maggot (Grub)

The cuterebra is a type of fly whose larvae infect the skin of animals. When the eggs hatch, the larva of the fly makes its own cocoon in the tissues just under the skin. You can see a swelling of about one-half inch under the skin of the head, neck, or trunk, with a perfectly round hole—the air hole for the larva—at its center.

An experienced veterinarian who recognizes the classic swelling with a perfect bore hole in the center makes the diagnosis easily. Treatment entails removing the larva from the skin. I usually do this by infusing the crater with a local anesthetic, opening the hole sufficiently to pull the larva out, and then flushing out the crater with antiseptic solution. I then put kitten on oral antibiotics to guard against infection.

Disease Info Box

Disease	Cuterebra maggot
Common Symptoms	$\frac{1}{2}$-inch swelling with hole in center
Diagnosis	Seeing the larva in crater
Treatment Options	Larva removal, flush, oral antibiotics

Fleas and Ticks

Let me start this section by saying that fleas and ticks are perhaps the most annoying bugs with which anyone should have to work. They both are external parasites of animals, and kittens get their share of them. I discuss each one in turn, covering life cycle, control, and treatment.

Fleas

The scientific name for the flea is *ctenocephalides*. All of us know how annoying these little bugs are. They've been a nuisance to man for the duration of written history—and probably before that, too.

All fleas are easily visible to the naked eye. They're about the size of sesame seeds, brownish red, and run very fast. When off the cat, they can jump six feet in one hop. They generally stay on the surface of the skin and run through the fur. Kittens pick them up by going outside in a grassy area or from another cat who has them. The four stages of the flea's 30-day life cycle are the egg, larvae, pupae, and adult, and are described in the following list:

- **Egg.** The egg is white, oval, and glossy. You can see the eggs with a magnifying glass. One female can lay hundreds of eggs during her life.

- **Larvae.**   The larvae is what emerges from the egg. These look like small worms, and can be seen with a magnifying glass. The final stage of the larva spins a cocoon, becoming a pupa. These cocoons usually are found in carpet fibers or under furniture.

- **Pupae.**   The flea undergoes changes in the cocoon as it transforms into an adult. This process is quite variable, and can take weeks to months. Vibration of the floor can stimulate the adult to hatch out of the cocoon and look for a host.

- **Adult.**   The adults are what most of us see on our kittens. Common sites at which to find the fleas are between the legs, the underside of the abdomen, and the inner thighs. Their feces are black specks we call "flea dirt." The adults are the only form that bite the pet. Adult fleas can live for longer than a month under the right conditions.

Fleas can reproduce very quickly; in fact, several adults can multiply into a couple thousand in one month! Your pets, house, and sometimes family members all become infected with these bloodsucking bugs. Occasionally they wander to other areas, but they don't stay long. The common site for flea bites on people is the ankle.

Not only do these bugs cause itching and allergic dermatitis, but they can carry disease. The cat flea can carry the tapeworm. Therefore, any kitten infested with fleas should be tested or treated for tapeworms (Chapter 2, "First Visit to the Veterinarian's" includes a discussion of tapeworm).

Treatment for fleas is twofold: it involves treating the cat *and* his environment. Treating only one doesn't break the life cycle, and if you don't break the life cycle, you won't get rid of the flea problem.

Treating Your Kitten for Fleas

The first thing most people do when they see fleas is give their kitten a flea bath, which is fine for killing the adult fleas. But this is only part of the problem. What about the eggs and larvae on the cat? What about the eggs and larvae in the house? What about the adults in the house? For now, let's concentrate on the pet.

When you treat your kitten, be sure to use a product that's safe for kittens. The labels tell you what is and isn't. All flea-killing formulas contain certain active ingredients. The most common are described below so you can know what you're using. This information is relevant regardless of the brand.

High potency active ingredients:
Carbamates (carbaryl)

Organophosphates (chlorpyrifos, cythioate, diazanon, dichlorvos, fenvalerate, fenthion, methylcarbamate, butoxypropylene, piperonyl butoxide, malathion)

Rotenone

You shouldn't use products that contain these ingredients on kittens. They're too strong and can have toxic side effects.

Moderate potency active ingredients:

Pyrethrin

Microencapsulated pyrethrin

Allethrin

Synergized pyrethroids

You could use some of these preparations in kittens as young as 6 weeks. They're mild, very effective, and have few side effects, but kill only adult fleas.

Mildest potency active ingredients:

Orange peel derivatives (D-limonene, Linalool)

You can use these on kittens as young as 6 weeks of age. They're very mild and prolonged contact with the flea is required needed to kill; they're more effective as flea repellents. Kills only adults.

Insect growth regulators:

Methoprene

Fenoxycarb

Prevents the normal progression of the flea's life cycle. In effect, prevents egg and/or larva from becoming an adult. Most of the female fleas lay eggs on the cat, so if the egg encounters a growth regulator prior to falling off, it doesn't develop or hatch in the house. Safe for kittens as young as 8 weeks old. Used worldwide in drinking water to reduce mosquito population. Used very effectively in combination with an adulticide for controlling recurrent flea infestations. Unusual to see any insect resistance.

Home remedies:

Brewer's yeast

Garlic cloves

Menthol

Eucalyptus

Herbal extracts

Many people swear by these all-natural formulations, despite little scientific evidence that they work. They're more of a repellent than an insecticide. You can use on kittens as young as 6 weeks old.

Flea control products come in a variety of forms, ranging from shampoos to sprays to powders to collars to dips to mousse foam. Each vet or groomer has a personal preference about which ones to use. Ask their advice or experiment to see what works best on your kitten.

A recent addition to the family of flea products is lufenuron, a once-a-month paste that contains insect development inhibitor, which causes the flea to become sterile when it bites, thus breaking the flea life cycle. This means that the eggs the female flea lays don't develop normally. I consider this more flea control for your house; it doesn't prevent fleas from living on and biting your kitten. But at least they can't breed and infest your house!

Another new products is *Imidacloprid*, a liquid applied to the scruff of the neck. The manufacturers claim it kills adult fleas within 24 hours and continues killing for three to four weeks. Fleas don't have time to lay eggs before they die. Since the product is topical, the manufacturers claim it has a wide margin of safety.

Guidelines for Flea Product Usage

1. Always follow the label directions on all flea products. Don't assume one product is like another.

2. Be careful to use products that are FDA-approved for use in kittens, not just adult cats. Most labels list the minimum age of cat on which the product is safe to use.

3. Use the product only as frequently as the label says. If it says to apply once weekly, then apply it weekly but no more often than that.

4. Follow all the hazard warning label instructions. Some products require the administrator to wear gloves or eye protection. Also, almost all of these products have child hazard warnings. So be careful and follow all warnings.

5. Treat all the animals in the house on the same day. Unfortunately, staggering the animals doesn't work.

6. If you like to see a "quick kill" of the adult fleas, shampoos and dips work the best.

7. If your kitten doesn't cooperative for a bath, then sprays, powder, topical products or mousse are the answer. These don't require you to soak the animal with anything. Usually a gentle misting, powdering, or foaming

over the entire animal except the face is all that's needed. Rub the spray into the coat after application to get it down to the skin level at which the fleas live.

8. Use insect growth regulators whenever possible to break the reproductive cycle of the adult fleas.

Treating the House for Fleas

Many products can kill fleas. Do not use products designed for the premise, or house, on your cat. This might be confusing to you at first, especially if you notice that the active ingredients are the same as in the cat products. The difference usually relates to concentration levels. The sprays for premises contain active ingredients in a concentration far too heavy to use safely on pets.

Fewer products are available for treating the house than for treating pets. The better products contain active ingredients to kill the adults, as well as insect growth regulators. They also boast long residuals (up to a year). Most of these products are for people to treat their own house. The alternative is to have an exterminator professionally treat your home.

Most people find exterminating fleas a major headache. The process can be very involved if you have multiple pets or a large living space to treat. I can tell you with certainty: If you don't follow the appropriate steps in a timely fashion, you won't get rid of your flea problem. If you've been through this process to no avail, you might want to consult a professional exterminator. Most give guarantees.

The most common reasons for failure in treating your flea problem are as follows:

- You didn't treat the pets *at the same time* as the house (this is the number one reason).
- You didn't treat all pets in the house *at the same time*.
- You used ineffective products, perhaps owing to resistance of the flea to the active ingredient.
- You didn't use enough product to effectively kill the fleas. *Follow directions!*
- You didn't bother to move furniture when applying a product for the house. You *must* get under *all* furniture.
- You didn't treat your kitten thoroughly enough. The product must reach all areas (except eyes), including the flea's favorite hangouts, the toes, behind ears, under tail, and between legs.

Guidelines for Home Treatments

- Always follow the label directions on all flea products. Don't assume one product is like another.

- Be careful to use products FDA approved for use in homes. Most labels list the appropriate surfaces on which the product is safe to use (drapes, upholstery, wood floors, rugs, and so on).

- Use the product only as frequently as the label says.

- Follow all the hazard warning label instructions. Some products require the administrator to wear gloves, or eye protection. Also, almost all of these products have child hazard warnings. So be careful and follow all warnings.

- All rooms where the kitten goes should be treated. The excuse, "my cat only eats in that room" doesn't matter. If the kitten goes into the room, treat the room.

- Start by vacuuming all the flooring and carpets in the house, and that means under furniture and baseboards, too. Throw out the vacuum bag afterwards, so you're not harboring fleas in your vacuum.

- Launder all pet bedding. This is a favorite place for fleas to live and eggs to hatch. If you can't launder it, throw it out.

- Remove all small items from the room, like plants, baskets, towel racks, pillows, and so on. The fewer items, the better the product can infiltrate.

- Try to use products that contain both an adulticide and an insect growth regulator. You want to kill both the adults and the eggs! Otherwise, you have to repeat all this over again in 3–4 weeks.

- The best time to do this is when the pets, people, and kids are out of the house. You should treat all pets for fleas at the same time, either outside, or at your local veterinarian's office or groomer.

- Leave enough time for this. It doesn't pay to rush the procedure. Remember, haste makes waste. If you forget a step, or don't cover the entire area, you end up repeating everything all over again in a few weeks, or sooner.

- Your veterinarian will be most happy to help you with your flea problem, so ask plenty of questions. He or she probably has a recommended system for flea control, including the necessary products. Vets are professionals in flea control.

- You used a product that didn't contain an insect growth regulator, and so managed to kill only adults. All those eggs in the rug and floor crevices still went ahead and hatched.

- You used an outdated product. Check for expiration dates.

- You forgot to throw away the vacuum bag after vacuuming for fleas. In effect, you made a flea hotel in your vacuum.

Ticks

Ticks are small wingless insects that normally live outdoors. They vary in size from a poppy seed to a large grape, depending on the stage, species, and state of engorgement (how much blood they've consumed). They're true parasites, in that they feed by sucking blood from the host. They've been around since the beginning of time. The tick life cycle involves four stages, as described in the following list:

- **Egg.** Females lay eggs in single batches of thousands, in the environment, not on the host. The eggs hatch into larvae in several weeks.

- **Larvae.** The larva hatches from the egg and finds a warm-blooded host. It feeds once for several days, then drops off into the environment and molts into a nymph stage tick.

- **Nymph.** This stage also needs to feed on a warm-blooded host. After feeding for about a week, it drops off to molt. This process can take months. But, once it's done, an adult emerges. The nymph can carry the disease.

- **Adult.** The adult tick is the product of a lengthy process that takes place over the course of months and involves three moltings and cooperation from three different hosts! Adult ticks can live for nearly two years. They carry tick-borne diseases.

Ticks are often found in certain locales, or geographic *pockets*. One neighborhood might be crawling with them, while the adjacent area might not have any. Why? These insects thrive in certain environmental conditions, namely damp and shady areas. Sunny pastures or dry land might not be able to sustain their life-cycle. Wooded, grassy, and thickly settled land with shrubs are perfect areas to find ticks.

Ticks are natural climbers. After they land on a cat, they climb upward until they reach the head and neck (unless they get lost on the way, which sometimes happens). This explains why most ticks are found on the head, especially the ears and eyelids.

After the tick settles into a comfortable spot, it "bites" the pet. This involves inserting its barbed long nose into the cat's skin to feed. The barbs make the apparatus operate along the lines of a fish hook, which makes removing these tenacious little bugs difficult. Chapter 5, "First Aid and Household Hazards," gives instructions for removing a tick.

Tick Products

Most of the information regarding flea products pertain to ticks, but not all. You must read labels. If a product is approved by the FDA for ticks, it says so on the label. Most products have a minimum age requirement. Generally speaking, the stronger the active ingredient, the older the kitten needs to be, sometimes up to 4–6 months old.

Disease Info Box

Disease	Fleas and ticks
Common Symptoms	Insects crawling on skin, allergic reaction
Diagnosis	Observation of the insects on their droppings
Treatment Options	Insecticidal products

Mange

Mange is the scientific word for microscopic mites that live in the skin of animals (and sometimes people). These bugs can cause a variety of symptoms ranging from intense itching and skin rash to hair loss and bacterial infection. Chapter 3, "Health Maintenance," includes a discussion of ear mites. The other types of mange that affect kittens are described in the following list:

- **Cheyletiella.** These mites live on the surface of the skin and don't burrow. They run along the surface of the epidermis, causing excessive flaking along the back of the kitten, hence the monikor, "Walking Dandruff." These bugs are very fragile and die quickly if they can't find a host animal. They're extremely contagious and spread quickly from a mother cat to all her kittens.

  Your vet treats mange by performing a *skin scraping* exam. A scraping of the skin is taken, placed on a slide with a drop of mineral oil, then examined under a microscope. The veterinarian can identify a mite by its looks. Treatment to kill the mites is done with every-other-day flea and tick shampoos. The insecticide that kills the flea and tick also kills cheyletiella. All animals in contact with the kitten should be checked for mange. *This mite can infect people*.

- **Demodex.** A cigar-shaped mite that lives in hair follicles. The one that infects cats is *demodex cati*, which causes intense itching and hair loss. Common affected sites on the kitten are the eyelids, around the eyes and face, or on the head. Small lesions often spread quickly, so a quick diagnosis is important. Your veterinarian performs a skin scraping to identify the mite. Treatment varies for this mite from that for cheyletiella. Special dips (weekly) and topical creams (daily) are used. This mite doesn't have public health significance.

- **Scabies.** The cat scabies, or *sarcoptic mange* mite, is *notoedres cati*, and is specific to cats. This is by far the most serious mange in animals. These mites burrow deep into the skin of cats, causing intense itching, red rash, hair loss, crusts, skin infection, and can lead to systemic disease. This mite is very contagious to other cats. Diagnosis is made the same way as for other types of mange, via a skin scraping. Treatment is more aggressive with sarcoptic mange, requiring special dips and injectable medications.

Disease Info Box	
Disease	Mange
Common Symptoms	Itching, hair loss, skin infections
Diagnosis	Skin scraping
Treatment Options	Dips, creams, Ivermectin injections

Paronychia

Paronychia is a condition in which you find inflammation and infection at the base of a nail. Since kittens are always scratching things, like plants and soiled litter in the litter box, they are prone to getting infections of the nail bed. With paronychia, swelling occurs around the base of the nail, and is very painful. You might even notice a discharge of blood or pus. Bacterial infection is common, but yeast infections also are possible. The nail can fall out, but often regrows. Diagnosis is made with history of painful toe and limping, swollen base of nail, with or without discharge, and/or nail loss. Treatment is relatively easy and involves soaking the paw in antiseptic foot baths, as well as giving oral and topical antibiotic or antifungal medications.

Disease Info Box

Disease	Paronychia
Common Symptoms	Limping, swollen base of nail, discharge
Diagnosis	Clinical observation, swollen nail, pain
Treatment Options	Foot soaks, antibiotics, antifungal medication

Pyoderma

Pyoderma is a deep skin infection. A kitten's skin is very thin and prone to scratches and cuts. Cats can get superficial scrapes and cuts as well, but these usually heal with a little help from you, by washing with hydrogen peroxide and topical antibiotic ointment. Deeper cuts often lead to deeper infection that requires veterinary care.

With such a cut, you'll notice red, inflamed skin and, often, a discharge and odor, as well as pus possibly oozing from open sores. These kittens run fevers and often feel sick and lethargic. They might not be eating. Your veterinarian probably will run a culture and sensitivity test to find out what bacteria is growing and the antibiotic with which treatment would be appropriate. Two of the most commonly cultured bacteria are the *staphylococcus* and *streptococcus* species.

If cultures come back negative, that is, no bacteria grew, three explanations are possible:

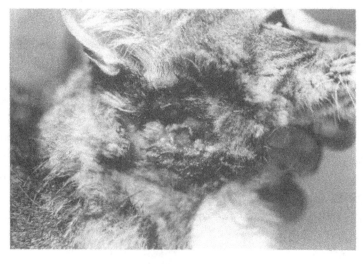

Superficial scrapes can lead to pyoderma, a deep infection, like this one on the cheek.

- The kitten was already on antibiotics
- The culture was done improperly or handled by the lab—perhaps try again
- The bacteria doesn't normally grow on a standard culture test—they might be anaerobic (requiring a special culture) or they might be the bacteria of a variety of other feline skin diseases, like *leprosy*, which also don't normally grow in a standard culture. Leprosy in cats looks like pyoderma, but the cultures are negative, and the skin develops large nodules and swelling that break open and drain.

Treatment of routine pyoderma involves antiseptic baths and soakings, appropriate oral antibiotics determined from the culture report, and supportive measures, like vitamins and extra nutrition. Most of these cases do respond well as long as another contributing factor isn't involved, like feline leukemia virus or feline immunodeficiency virus, or a heavy burden of internal parasites.

Disease Info Box

Disease	Pyoderma
Common Symptoms	Open skin sores, skin draining pus, fever
Diagnosis	Skin cultures
Treatment Options	Medicated baths, oral antibiotics, vitamins

Ringworm Fungus

Ringworm is a fungal disease of the skin of animals and people. We all know about fungus because we have all seen moldy bread or mildew in our showers, but those don't infect us. Ringworm fungus grows on skin, causing disease. The name of the fungus species that infects cats is called *microsporum*. It can also infect dogs and humans. Cats contract ringworm from contact with another infected animal.

Symptoms can take weeks to develop, but once they do, they're hard to miss: hair loss, crusting in a circular lesion, intensely itchy, and irritated. The crusty spots grow and spread, usually over the head and neck areas. The fungus also spreads in the hair that falls out and can live for up to a year in the environment. Cats often carry the ringworm fungus in their coat without showing symptoms. That doesn't mean they won't spread it around to everyone else, though!

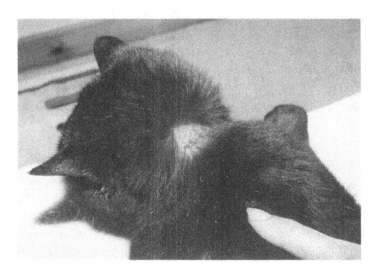

Ringworm leads to loss of hair and crusting.

Diagnosis is made by identifying the fungus on the skin, in one of two ways:

- Running a fungal culture to identify the species of fungus
- Examining the kitten's coat with a black UV light, called a *Woods Lamp* (ringworm fungus fluoresces a brilliant green under a UV light)

Treatment consists of shaving lesions and applying antifungal cream; shampooing with antifungal shampoos; or, for severe cases, oral antifungal medication.

There is a vaccine to protect against ringworm in cats, which also has been used to treat cases of ringworm. Ask your vet about it for your kitten. You will need to treat your house, also, because the fungus lives on the shed hair for months. Clean all surfaces where cat hair falls with a disinfectant that kills mold. Vacuum all the loose hair, then wash all surfaces. *Note:* Consult your doctor for advice about your own health concerns.

Disease Info Box

Disease	Ringworm fungus
Common Symptoms	Circular raised hairless itchy lesions
Diagnosis	Fungal culture and Woods Lamp exam
Treatment Options	Antifungal baths, creams, oral medications, vaccine

Rodent Ulcer (and Eosinophilic Plaque)

The name sounds horrible, but the disease isn't too bad. A *rodent ulcer* is a thickening or swelling of the mucus membranes of the mouth, especially the lips. An *eosinophilic plaque or granuloma* is very similar, except it occurs in the skin of the abdomen and thighs. These ulcers and plaques can be itchy. The cause generally is considered to be an allergic reaction that leads to swelling of the tissues.

Basically, a rodent ulcer or plaque is a large, elongated hive that can last for weeks. Females seem more prone to these ulcers. It's very important for your veterinarian to distinguish a rodent ulcer or plaque from cancer, infection, or trauma. Sometimes the only way to correctly diagnose these cases is to biopsy the swelling.

Treatment is twofold: identify and remove the cause of the allergy, and use anti-inflammatory drugs like cortisone to reduce the swelling and itching. I have patients who have rodent ulcers and plaques that flare up from time to time, requiring cortisone injections. We cannot always identify the causative agent, but they're often seasonal. These swellings are only of concern if they occur in the throat, where they can interfere with breathing.

Disease Info Box

Disease	Rodent ulcer and eosinophilic plaques
Common Symptoms	Raised thickenings of lips or skin of thighs
Diagnosis	Biopsy
Treatment Options	Cortisone medicaiton, allergy testing

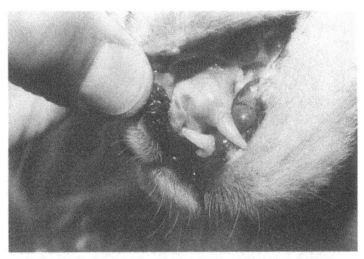

A rodent ulcer is a large, elongated bump in the mouth.
The kitten's lower fang has punctured the swelling.

Seborrhea (dry and oily)

Seborrhea is a condition in which excessive skin flakes off, leaving severe dandruff (in the dry form) or large, waxy crusts (in the oily form). The dry form is far more common in cats. Persian cats have an incurable form of inherited oily seborrhea. These kittens constantly have oily coats despite frequent bathing. Common causes of seborrhea are as follows:

- Overly frequent bathing or using the wrong shampoo
- Nutritional deficiencies, especially fatty acid deficiency
- Intestinal parasites
- Skin diseases like mange or fleas
- Infrequent or inadequate grooming
- Indoor climate conditions that are too warm or too dry

Diagnosis is easy for an experienced veterinarian. The owners usually tell tales of severe itching and some hair loss. Treatment usually involves more frequent grooming, anti-seborrhea shampoos, additional fatty acids in the diet, and humectant moisturizers.

Disease Info Box

Disease	Seborrhea
Common Symptoms	Dry, flaky, itchy skin, sever dandruff
Diagnosis	Poor coat, lack of other diseases
Treatment Options	Medicated shampoos, moisturizers, fatty acids

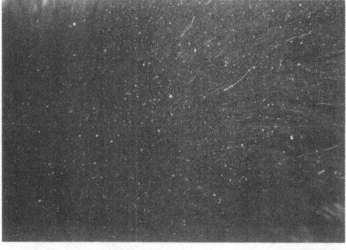

An example of dry seborrhea. Notice the severe dandruff flaking.

Solar Dermatitis (Sunburn)

You might be wondering how a furry cat can get sunburned. The answer is that most don't. But white cats are susceptible, especially on the face and ear tips. Pure white cats that live in southern climates that offer maximum sun exposure shouldn't be outdoor cats. Sunburn looks the same in white cats as it does in fair-skinned people—redness, blistering, bleeding, and pain. The diagnosis can be confused with anything that burns skin, such as chemical burns, or thermal burns. In the absence of any other factor, sunburn is the obvious diagnosis. Treatment is aimed at reducing the pain and inflammation, as well as guarding against secondary infection. This usually involves cortisone anti-inflammatory drugs as well as antibiotic skin creams.

Unfortunately, with repeated sun exposure and sunburn, white cats are particularly susceptible to skin cancer—not melanoma like us, but *squamous cell carcinoma*. These skin cancers show up as ulcerated skin sores that don't heal and bleed often. Only a skin biopsy can confirm the presence of skin cancer. Surgical removal of the cancer is recommended along with other anti-cancer therapies, like chemotherapy.

Disease Info Box

Disease	Solar dermatitis (sunburn)
Common Symptoms	Red, bleeding, blistered skin of ears or face
Diagnosis	Burns with no other apparent cause, biopsy
Treatment Options	Cortisone and antibiotic skin creams, keep indoors

Stud Tail

Stud tail is a condition in which the male cat, beginning at adolescence, develops an active oil gland (called the *Preen* or *Supra caudal* gland) at the base of his tail. The skin and fur around the gland becomes greasy, thick with blackheads, swollen, red, and possibly, infected. Your veterinarian can quickly recognize this condition in sexually active male cats. Treatment aims to reduce the inflammation, soak up excess oils, and prevent infection. You can wash out the oils with soap and water, or dry them up by sprinkling corn starch, leaving it overnight, then brushing it out. You can reduce inflammation by using anti-inflammatory drugs, such as topical cortisone, and warm compresses. Use antibiotics to guard against infection. Chapter 3, "Health Maintenance," explains grooming considerations for this condition.

Disease Info Box

Disease	Stud Tail
Common Symptoms	Oily, inflamed skin at base of tail
Diagnosis	Inflamed Preen gland
Treatment Options	Corn starch, warm compresses, soap washing, cortisone, antibiotic creams, extra grooming habits

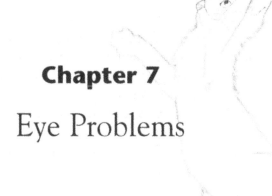

Chapter 7

Eye Problems

This chapter covers the most common eye afflictions of kittens. The eyes are extremely sensitive organs, prone to injury and disease because they are prominent and not well protected, especially for kittens who are forever sticking their noses into everything.

Eyes are susceptible to injury, getting foreign material in them, scratches, getting poked, and disease. Wow, that sounds like a lot. The good news is that eyes also are very resilient and can heal quickly. Let's go through some of the most common eye problems of kittens.

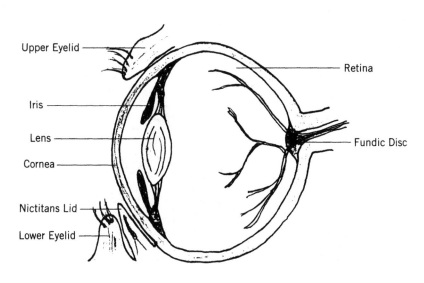

Anatomy of the kitten's eye.

Blocked Tear Ducts

What is a tear duct, you ask? Another word for the tear duct is the *lacrimal duct*, which is the thin tube that carries tears, produced with each blink of the eye, from the corner of the eye and into the nose. Kittens can be born with a closed tear duct, though this is rare, and most common in breeds with pushed-in faces, like Persians and Himalayans.

A closed duct prevents tears from draining normally into the nose. Where else can they go? They just stream down the corners of the eye and face, causing *tear staining*. Tear staining of the fur usually is a rusty brown color, not to be confused with dried blood.

Other than being born with defective tear ducts, any infection of the eye, like conjunctivitis in young kittens, can permanently damage the tear duct by obstructing it. Diagnosis is made by observing the stream of tears down the face. Treatment isn't always necessary, but if you have a valuable show cat, a veterinary ophthalmologist might be able to perform one of several surgical techniques for opening the duct and thereby eliminating the tear staining.

Disease Info Box

Disease	Blocked tear duct
Common Symptoms	Constant tearing and staining in corner of eye
Diagnosis	Clinical presentation
Treatment Options	Washing face, surgery

This kitten has blocked tear ducts. Notice the dark tear stains. *Dr. M. Neaderland*

Cataracts (Juvenile)

A *cataract* is a defective lens of the eye that is no longer transparent. It becomes opaque so that the animal cannot see through it. You see it as a white pearl in the center of the eye. This differs from cataracts that develop after eight years of age. Kittens are born with juvenile cataracts, or they show up within the first year. Your veterinarian can see the opacity with a special ophthalmic tool called a *slit lamp*, which projects a narrow slit of bright light that penetrates into the lens, highlighting the cataract. Most of these cataracts don't affect vision. Occasionally some worsen and get larger and more opaque, and can potentially interfere with normal vision. This progression can take years. At that point, surgery can be performed to remove the defective lens, restoring vision.

Disease Info Box	
Disease	Juvenile cataract
Common Symptoms	Pearl-like opacity in the eye
Diagnosis	Slit lamp exam
Treatment Options	None, surgical removal if needed

Conjunctivitis

Conjunctivitis is a disease in which the tissues surrounding the eye become infected or inflamed. Symptoms include redness, swelling, itching or burning, squinting, and thick eye discharge. The kitten often paws at his eyes or rubs them on the carpet. Conjunctivitis can be very annoying for a young kitten, but it's young kittens who are most susceptible to it. The third eyelid (*nictitans membrane*) often is raised in times of eye disease. We call this having the *haws*. Conjunctivitis has many different causes, including three basic types— viral, bacterial, and allergic. Let's look at each one separately.

- **Viral conjunctivitis.** Chapter 2 already mentioned two viruses that can cause conjunctivitis in kittens: feline rhinotracheitis and feline calicivirus. The conjunctivitis of these viruses is a part of having an upper respiratory infection (URI). The hallmarks of viral URI include excessive clear, watery eye tearing and sneezing, which can go on for weeks. Antibiotic therapy helps prevent it from progressing to bacterial bronchitis, or sinus infection, but cannot cure the virus. The kitten's immune system has to take care of the virus.

A kitten with viral conjunctivitis.

- **Bacterial conjunctivitis.** Several bacteria can infect the kitten's eyes. As with viral conjunctivitis, the eyes become very red and swollen, but unlike viral cases, the discharge is thick and yellow. The eyes might crust shut. These kittens could run a fever and seem lethargic. Also unlike viral cases, upper respiratory symptoms usually aren't present. The conjunctiva can become so swollen that it billows out. The third eyelid usually protrudes and can show raised white plaques. The bacteria that are most commonly infect kitten eyes are *chlamydia*, *mycoplasma*, and *staphylococcus*.

- **Allergic conjunctivitis.** Kittens who have allergies to airborne contaminants, like dust or pollen, can have swollen, itchy, watery eyes, with excessive clear, watery tears, sneezing, and often itching of the face, eyes, and muzzle. The big difference in allergic and infectious conjunctivitis is that kittens with allergies act fine, have no fever, and show symptoms only during exposure to the allergen.

Diagnosing conjunctivitis involves differentiating between the three different types. Your vet needs to take a complete history, run a culture, and perform a thorough exam. Bacterial and viral conjunctivitis are contagious to other cats, so isolate your kitten. Treatment depends on the type of conjunctivitis. Viral and bacterial conjunctivitis usually involve prolonged topical eye drops or ointment. See Chapter 6, "Special Health Concerns," for how to administer them.

Sometimes oral antibiotics are given for bacterial conjunctivitis. If you must do this, you need to clean the eyes several times a day with warm water or eye wash to keep them from crusting closed. The allergic type means having to identify the allergy and treat it. See the section on miliary dermatitis in Chapter 7, "Skin Diseases," for a more complete description of allergies in kittens.

Disease Info Box	
Disease	Conjunctivitis
Common Symptoms	Swollen, red, itchy eyes with discharge
Diagnosis	Physical exam, cultures, allergy testing
Treatment Options	Ophthalmic medication, oral antibiotics

Corneal Sequestration of Persians

This is a peculiar disease that primarily strikes the eyes of Persians and Siamese. The center of the cornea dies off, leaving a black, necrotic (dead) center. The main symptoms are redness and inflamed eyes, squinting, new blood vessels growing into the cornea, watery eye discharge, and a black spot in the center of the cornea. An experienced vet diagnoses this disease easily by recognizing the breed, symptoms, and chronic nature of the disease. Treatment requires a qualified veterinary ophthalmologist to surgically remove the dead black center. The surgery is called a *superficial keratectomy*. It's a tricky procedure because the necrotic center goes deep, so removal runs the risk of going through

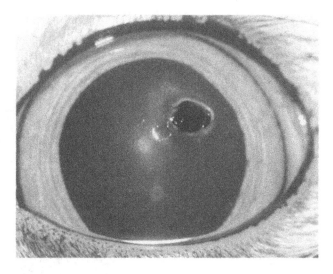

The black dead spot on this kitten's cornea is a sequestration. *Dr. M. Neaderland*

the cornea and rupturing the eye. The surgeon then sutures the eye closed so that the cornea can heal. After reopening the eye, antibiotic ophthalmic medications are used. Finally, after the entire cornea is healed, ophthalmic cortisone is applied to reduce scarring.

Disease Info Box

Disease	Corneal sequestration
Common Symptoms	Red eye, tearing, squinting, black corneal center
Diagnosis	Exam of eye, chronic nature, black cornea
Treatment Options	Superficial keratectomy

Corneal Ulceration and Abrasions

Simple things like cat fights, getting scratched or poked in the eye, or an infectious disease can cause an ulcer, or crater-like defect in the cornea. This defect is very painful—imagine having a piece of dirt in your eye, but you can't wash it out. The problem is that these corneal ulcers and scratches get infected very quickly. The kitten usually keeps the eye closed. Owing to the trauma, the pupils often are constricted, which is painful.

Your veterinarian makes the diagnosis by examining the eye for corneal defects. He first uses an ophthalmic topical anesthetic, then places a drop of an ophthalmic *fluorescein stain* in the eye. Next, he rinses the stain out. If a disruption

A kitten with a corneal ulcer.

has occurred in the superficial layer of the cornea (the cornea has five layers) the stain adheres to that affected area, highlighting the scratch or ulcer and allowing your veterinarian to easily visualize the defect.

Treatment basically entails letting the cornea heal itself, which it does quickly, as long as it remains free of infection and the ulcer doesn't run too deep. Antibiotic ophthalmic ointments are applied often, up to every hour as needed, to keep the ulcer from getting infected. *Never use an ointment that has cortisone in it, because cortisone can cause a delay in healing in the eye, making the ulcer worse.* All corneal ulcers need to be restained often, every two to three days, to access the progress.

Disease Info Box

Disease	Corneal ulcers and abrasions
Common Symptoms	Squinting, painful red eye, crater in cornea
Diagnosis	Fluorescein stain test
Treatment Options	Ophthalmic antibiotics, atropine, suture eye closed (in severe cases)

Cross-Eyed (Strabismus)

Cross-eyed describes a deviation of one or both eyes. It affects Siamese cats, Himalayans, Birmans, Toniknese, and other Asian breeds. The strabismus is caused by a variation of the optic nerve. No treatment is necessary and most of these cats don't seem to have any sight problems.

This cross-eyed kitten has what is technically known as a strabismus.
Christine Appleman

Dry Eye (Keratoconjunctivitis Sicca)

Some cats have a reduced or complete absence of natural tear production. Tears are essential to keeping the cornea well lubricated and moist. With every blink of the eye, a tear film coats the cornea; without sufficient tears, the cornea dries out. If the cornea dries out, it becomes inflamed. Both eyes often are afflicted. The body tries to lubricate the eye by secreting pus from the conjunctiva, which is woefully inadequate. Ultimately, blindness sets in. Your vet diagnoses keratoconjuctivitis sicca by actually measuring the tear production of both eyes. Treatment for dry eye is twofold and usually necessary for the rest of your kitten's life:

1. Add artificial tear drops or ointment frequently to replace absent tears

2. Apply ophthalmic medications, including *cyclosporine*, which increases the natural production of tears

Entropion

This is a condition in which the eyelid—usually the lower, rolls inward so that the lower eye lashes rub right on the cornea (surface of the eye). Entropion is *congenital*, meaning, present at birth, and usually afflicts Persians. The kittens have a constantly tearing eye, squint or hold the eye half closed, and show redness. Diagnosis is easy. Your veterinarian has to observe the rolling in of the eyelid. Mild cases can be treated with ophthalmic lubricants to reduce the rubbing. More severe cases need surgical correction. The most common procedure is called the *pinch technique*, where a slit of skin is removed to cause the eyelid to roll outward. Think of it as an eyelid tuck.

Haws

Haws are the prolapsed third eyelids of cats. All cats have three eyelids: upper, lower, and third (also called the *nictitans membrane*). These eyelids provide extra protection for the eyes. They come up in times of stress, or during periods of eye irritation. They should retract when the stress or irritation is over. In some kittens, they stay up, for the following three main reasons:

- Prolonged or chronic eye irritation
- Certain drugs, like tranquilizers and anesthetics
- Systemic disease and dehydration

Most cases of haws that I see trace back to systemic illness, such as feline leukemia virus, feline immunodeficiency virus, severe internal parasites, dehydration, and fever. The last case I saw of haws was Lyme disease, which is unusual in cats. Some veterinarians treat the haws with eye drops that temporarily retract the third eyelids. I would rather look for the primary cause and cure that.

Iris Freckles

Many people notice color differentiations, or spots, on the iris of their kitten's eyes. These are just freckles and shouldn't be of any concern or require any treatment, as long as the freckles are small, flat, don't deform the iris, and don't change. Freckles should not be confused with tumors of the iris, which are large, irregular shapes that deform the iris.

Proptosis

Proptosis is when the eyeball is literally knocked out of its socket—usually during blunt trauma to the head. If sufficient stretching and trauma occur to the optic nerve or blood vessels, permanent visual impairment can result. The best thing your veterinarian can do is assess whether he can save the eye.

Retinal Diseases

The retina is the back layer of the eye which receives light through the lens, then converts light images into nerve impulses that go to the brain. As you can imagine, the retina is crucial for normal vision. No retina, no vision—it's that simple. Retinal diseases are diagnosed with an eye exam that includes visualization of the back of the eye (retina) and a *fundic* exam, which visualizes the central zone where the optic nerve enters the eye (fundus). The three most common retinal diseases of kittens are as follows:

- **Inherited Retinal Disease.**   As the name says, the kitten inherits the disease from the parents. Persians and Abyssinian cats are affected. Unfortunately, the retinas of these kittens progressively degenerate until they go blind. There is a progressive blindness and dilated pupils. As horrible as it sounds, many blind kittens live wonderful lives as long as you keep them inside and don't rearrange the furniture too often.

- **Retinal Detachment.**   This condition is when the retina actually becomes detached or peels away from the back of the eye, causing sudden blindness and dilated pupils. This can occur as a result of trauma

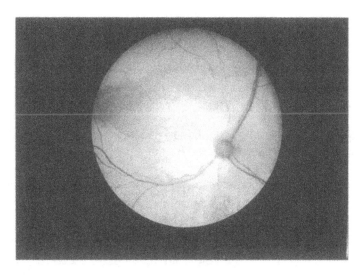

This is the retina of a kitten with central retinal degeneration. *Dr. M. Neaderland*

to the head, such as falling out of a tree or getting hit by a car. Some underlying diseases also can lead to retinal detachment, such as toxoplasmosis, feline infectious peritonitis, and some poisonings. Nothing much can be done to treat the condition, other than cage rest in hopes that the retina might reattach on its own, even partially. Any underlying disease must be treated, too.

- **Feline Central Retinal Degeneration (FCRD).**   This is a reversible retinal disease that actually stems from a nutritional deficiency. Both eyes are affected, and your veterinarian will find on physical exam degenerative changes to the retina, starting at the center. The cause is a deficiency of the amino acid *taurine*. Veterinarians don't see this disease often nowadays because most complete and balanced kitten foods include taurine.

Disease Info Box

Disease	Retinal disease
Common Symptoms	Sudden or progressive blindness, dilated pupils
Diagnosis	Retinal and fundic eye exam
Treatment Options	None for inherited, cage rest for detachment, taurine supplements for FCRD

Uveitis

Uveitis is an eye disease in which you see inflammation inside the eyeball. The inflammation can be severe and can cause temporary or permanent blindness. It has two main causes:

- Eye trauma
- Infectious diseases, like toxoplasmosis, feline infectious peritonitis, and roundworms

Trauma is the most common cause of uveitis. The symptoms of uveitis are suddenly painful and red eye; sensitivity to light; a small pupil; blood or pus inside eye; and squinting. Diagnosis is made when the above symptoms are seen in a cat who has a severely inflamed eye. Treatment aims to stop the inflammatory process quickly before more damage occurs to the inner structures of the eye. Potent anti-inflammatory drugs are used, such as cortisone, either as topical ophthalmic drops or injections.

Disease Info Box	
Disease	Uveitis
Common Symptoms	Red, painful eye, small pupil, blood in eye
Diagnosis	Eye exam, blood tests for underlining disease
Treatment Options	Cortisone, atropine, treat underlining disease

Chapter 8

Ear
Diseases

This chapter is a short one—few diseases affect your young kitten's ears. Ear mites are the most common ear affliction, and they're covered in Chapter 3, "Health Maintenance." The remaining ear problems are discussed in this chapter.

Aural Hematoma

Aural just means ear, and *hematoma* means blood clot. Put the two together, and you get a blood clot in the ear flap. To understand what really happens, you need to know the anatomy of the ear flap, which is where the hematoma occurs.

The ear flap (also called *pinna*) of a kitten is made of three layers: two layers of skin with a middle layer of cartilage. If a blood vessel in the ear flap leaks, blood oozes out and fills the space between the skin of the ear flap and the cartilage, causing a large, painful swelling, usually on the inside of the ear. Owners see this acute swelling and panic because it looks like something is ready to explode. The fact is the hematoma can stay for weeks to months. What causes a blood vessel to leak? Usually trauma, such as a cat fight, blunt trauma to the head, or violent shaking or scratching of the ears (due to ear mites).

Treatment consists of one of two techniques. The first is to aspirate the swelling with a needle and syringe to draw out as much of the fluid as you can. The problem with this technique is that the hematomas often fill back up again, only giving temporary relief from the swelling.

The second and more successful technique involves general anesthesia and lancing the hematoma. The fluid and blood clot are removed, the two layers of the skin are sutured together flat, and a small port hole is left open to allow further drainage. Systemic oral antibiotics are given to guard against infection, and any underlying cause should be treated.

Disease Info Box	
Disease	Aural hematoma
Common Symptoms	Large painful swelling of ear flap
Diagnosis	Physical exam, aspirate blood from it
Treatment Options	Needle aspiration, surgical lancing and suturing flat

Deafness (Congenital)

Most of us think of deafness as an old age change, and we'd be right. Newborn kittens who are white, and especially those with blue eyes, however, can enter the world with a congenital form of deafness. Deafness can occur in up to 20% of all white kittens. The actual mechanism is a defect in the development of the nerves that service the ear. The first thing the owners notice is that their kitten doesn't respond to normal household sounds—knocks at the door, phone ringing, people yelling, and so forth. Most people start testing their kitten by clapping their hands or banging pots behind the kitten's head when it doesn't seem to know they're there. Diagnosis is easy if it's a white kitten. Unfortunately, few diagnostic tests are available for assessing the degree of deafness.

There is no treatment, or hearing aid, for cats who have congenital deafness. You have to learn to use hand signals to get their attention. Just like any handicap, patience and tons of TLC are the answer.

Disease Info Box	
Disease	Deafness
Common Symptoms	No reaction to sound stimulus
Diagnosis	Trying clapping behind ears for reaction
Treatment Options	None, lots of TLC

Outer Ear Infection (Otitis Externa)

There are two types of otitis externa, bacterial and yeast. I cover each in turn.

Bacterial Otitis Externa

Bacteria can easily find its way into the external ear canal of kittens. Conditions that encourage bacterial contamination include living in dirty conditions, scratching ears with dirty hind toenails, and contamination with feces or urine. After the bacteria invades the ear canal, it causes inflammation, and usually pus formation. You would see this as a yellow, odiferous discharge.

Bacterial cultures are needed to identify the bacteria. *Staphylococcus* and *pseudomonas* are two common bacteria found in ears of cats. Treatment begins with a thorough flushing and cleaning of the ear canal to remove any debris. Topical ear antibacterial ointments usually are applied afterwards. In severe cases, oral antibiotics might be necessary. The best cure, of course, is prevention—just keep the ears clean and dry.

Yeast Otitis Externa

Yeast otitis externa infections are caused by a yeast rather than a bacteria, but otherwise is quite similar. The most common yeast cultured out of animal ears is *malassezia*. Yeast needs several conditions to grow: darkness, dampness, and a growth media, like ear wax. You can see that getting water or moisture in waxy ears predisposes them to yeast infections. There rarely is any discharge besides excess ear wax, which also is a symptom of ear mites, so you'll want the ear checked regardless.

The ear becomes very red and itchy, and usually has a very sour odor. Diagnosis is achieved by putting together the clinical signs, smelling the sour odor, and seeing excessive black wax. Treatment involves a thorough ear flushing

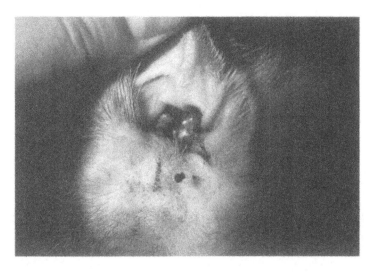

An example of otitis externa, or outer ear infection.

or cleaning to remove any debris and applying topical ear anti-yeast medications. Prevention, as in the bacterial form of the disease, entails keeping the ears clean and dry. This must be differentiated from ear mites, which can look very similar.

Disease Info Box	
Disease	Otitis externa
Common Symptoms	Red, inflamed, painful ear, shaking head, scratching
Diagnosis	Ear exam, bacterial or yeast culture
Treatment Options	Ear flush, topical antibiotic or anti-yeast medications

Chapter 9

Dental Diseases

C hapter 2, "First Visit to the Veterinarian's," describes the preventive and maintenance things you can do for your kitten's smile. This chapter looks at the most common dental diseases of kittens. Most of the diseases stem from tooth neglect, but one is a developmental problem, and I'll start with it first.

Retained Deciduous Teeth

Deciduous teeth are the baby kitten teeth that are designed to last only three to four months before they fall out and are replaced with permanent teeth. The timing of this dental change-over is crucial because the baby tooth needs to fall out on time so the permanent tooth can come in. If the deciduous tooth doesn't fall out soon enough, or at all, it can cause the permanent tooth to come in crooked, late (*impacted tooth*), or not at all. The diagnosis is easy for an experienced veterinarian to do an oral exam to determine which teeth are baby teeth and which are permanent. If all the deciduous teeth haven't fallen out by six months of age, you want to take your kitten to the vet. Table 9.1 gives the teething schedule.

Veterinarians typically extract any retained deciduous teeth when the kitten is spayed or neutered. This treatment allows permanent teeth to finally cut through.

Table 9.1 Kitten Teething Schedule		
Tooth	**Deciduous**	**Permanent**
Incisors	2–4 weeks	4 months
Canines	4 weeks	5 months
Premolars	2 months	4–5 months
Molars	none present	5 months

Disease Info Box

Disease	Retained deciduous teeth
Common Symptoms	Crooked, late, or impacted permanent teeth
Diagnosis	Oral exam
Treatment Options	Extraction of retained deciduous teeth by 6 months

Cracked Tooth

Kittens sometimes play too rough or pounce and bite down on hard objects, such as turtle shells, mouse bones, or hard play toys. Occasionally they crack a tooth. If the tooth is a deciduous kitten tooth, due to fall out anyway, you don't need to bother fixing the tooth. If it's bleeding or painful, the tooth should just be extracted. If the tooth is a permanent one, then your veterinarian needs to decide whether he can save the tooth or should extract it.

The most common scenario is a kitten who suddenly cracks a tooth and is bleeding. If you have the tooth treated right away, your vet might be able to save the tooth using a pulp cap. The bleeding signifies that the pulp cavity, the center of the tooth at which the nerve and blood vessels convege, is exposed to the outside air. If the pulp cavity isn't sealed, bacteria gets in and causes a tooth abscess. If a delay of days or weeks precedes treatment, and the tooth is damaged or infected already, the tooth most likely will need a root canal, or *endodontics* to relieve the pain, clean out the infection, and save the tooth. If all else fails, the tooth might need to be extracted, which isn't a serious problem.

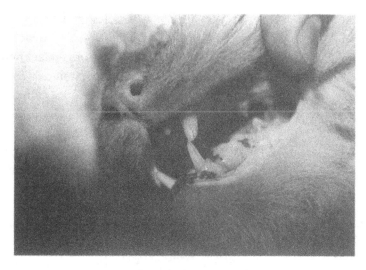

A cracked upper tooth.

Disease Info Box

Disease	Cracked tooth
Common Symptoms	Recently cracked, bleeding tooth
Diagnosis	Oral exam
Treatment Options	Pulp cap, root canal, extraction as a last resort

Gingivitis, Periodontal Disease, and Dental Tartar

Gingivitis is inflammation of the gums. *Periodontitis* is the inflammation of the tissues that surround the tooth. *Tartar* is a hard mineralized coating to teeth.

Many people think that they're being kind to their kitten by feeding them people food (like tuna) and canned kitten food. Chapter 4, "Feeding and Nutrition," explains why this isn't good for nutrition or dental hygiene.

Feeding an all-soft diet leads to excess plaque coating on teeth. Plaque is a film comprised of saliva, food

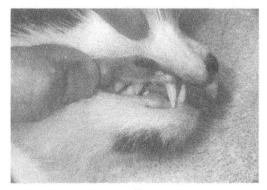

Normal, permanent kitten teeth. Notice the clean teeth and normal gums.

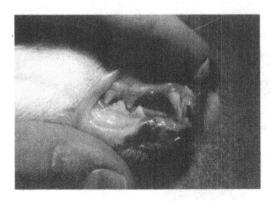

If you don't take regular care of your kitten's teeth, he could end up with severe tartar and gingivitis, like this cat.

particles, and bacteria. If the plaque isn't removed by brushing or regular chewing of hard food, it mineralizes into a hard coating, called tartar. Tartar, being hard, can push between the gums and the tooth, causing a pocket. More bacteria, plaque, and tartar then fill this pocket, pushing the gums further away from the tooth. Eventually, the root of the tooth becomes exposed. Bacteria can invade the roots of the tooth, causing inflammation of the tissues around the tooth root. This is called periodontal disease. Eventually, the bacteria causes an abscess (infection). Within a short time, the tooth is lost to infection and either falls out or needs to be extracted.

What a horrible scenario! Don't let it happen. Good dental hygiene and proper nutrition is essential to prevent gingivitis, periodontal disease, and tartar. See Chapter 3 for dental maintenance.

I should mention that in normal circumstances, kittens should not have gingivitis, periodontal disease, or tartar formation until they're at least one year old. If you see it in a young kitten, your veterinarian should suspect one of several diseases like feline leukemia virus, feline immunodeficiency virus, or severe parasitism. The vet can easily test for these diseases with a blood test or a stool exam.

Disease Info Box

Disease	Gingivitis, periodontal disease, tartar
Common Symptoms	Gum and tooth inflammation, hard coating to teeth (tartar)
Diagnosis	Oral exam, dental exam, FeLV-FIV test, stool test
Treatment Options	Dental cleaning, better dental hygiene, dry foods

Chapter 10

Mouth and Throat Diseases

J ust look inside your kitten's mouth to see all the different structures it contains:

- The roof of the mouth, or *hard palate*
- A tongue with the bristles for grooming
- Tonsils, which are lymph nodes the body uses to fight throat infections
- The throat, which can be red and swollen in times of disease

These organs are quite vulnerable to disease and infection because the mouth is a direct opening to the outside world and lets all kinds of stuff into a kitten's throat. Your veterinarian examines the mouth and throat of your kitten during every visit.

Cleft Palate

Cleft means fissure, or crack; the *palate* is the roof of the mouth. Put the two together, and you get a cracked roof of the mouth. That's a cleft palate in a nutshell, except the palate hasn't really cracked—it never fused together properly during fetal development. Sometimes the lip gets involved and you get a cleft lip along with the palate. The breed predisposition is in Siamese cats.

The first symptom owners notice is food or milk bubbling out of the nostrils while eating or drinking. Because of the hard palate (roof of the mouth) separates the mouth from the nasal passages, food and liquid leak directly into the nose, causing the bubbling of liquids as the kitten breaths. It also can lead to choking and coughing. The only treatment that really works is surgical repair, that is, closure of the cleft. The ideal time for this surgery is when the kitten is young—around nine to twelve weeks of age. Before that, you just need to be careful not to feed your kitten too many liquid diets, because these promote the choking and even aspiration of liquid foods into the lungs. If that happens, an *aspiration pneumonia* can develop, requiring treatment with oral antibiotics.

Disease Info Box	
Disease	Cleft palate
Common Symptoms	Bubbling of liquids and soft food from nostrils
Diagnosis	Oral exam
Treatment Options	Surgical correction of cleft, limit soft and liquid foods

Candidiasis

Candidiasis is a yeast infection of the mouth. Kittens who have been on oral antibiotics for long periods are susceptible to developing this yeast infection. The actual yeast is *candida albicans*. The fungus infects the mouth and throat of young kittens. The lesions produced by the fungus are raised white plaques with ulceration or blistering of the mucus membranes. These lesions can get large enough to cause severe pain and difficulty swallowing, which can cause a young kitten to stop eating. The best way to diagnose these cases is to use a fungal culture. Treatment is fairly simple, but twofold: stop the antibiotic therapy if you can, and use antifungal medications to kill the candida yeast.

Disease Info Box	
Disease	Candidiasis
Common Symptoms	Raised white plaques on roof of mouth that ulcerate
Diagnosis	Fungal culture, FeLV and FIV tests
Treatment Options	Discontinue oral antibiotics, anti-yeast medications

Oral Blisters (Viral Stomatitis)

You know what it's like to have a blister in your mouth. It hurts. In kittens, oral blisters come from viruses that infect the mucus membranes of the mouth. The word *stomatitis* means inflammation of the oral mucus membranes. The blisters can be anywhere in the mouth, on the tongue, or on the palate and gums. (Chapter 2, "First Visit to the Veterinarian's," covers all the viruses that cause blistering of the mouth in detail.) Affected kittens need special care, because most of them stop eating because of the pain associated with the blisters.

Your vet diagnoses the problem by running a panel of blood tests for the specific viruses. Usually one or more of them turns up positive. These kittens are contagious to other cats, so keep them away. Treatment and outcome varies, depending on which virus is the culprit.

Disease Info Box

Disease	Viral stomatitis
Common Symptoms	Oral and tongue blisters
Diagnosis	Oral exam, virus blood tests
Treatment Options	Supportive care, oral antibiotics and anti-viral drugs

Tonsillitis (Strep Throat)

This is one disease everybody knows about—maybe you even had your tonsils removed when you were a kid. Tonsillitis in kittens results from bacterial infection of the throat and *tonsil glands*, the lymph nodes that help guard against and fight infection in the throat. During infection, the tonsils become red, swollen, and tender, which leads to difficulty swallowing. In severe cases, pus and blood can ooze from the tonsils. These kittens are sick, run a fever of over 103°F, don't eat, gag a lot, and swallow heavily even when they're not eating.

The most common bacteria that infects the throats of animals and people is *streptococcus*, otherwise known as "strep throat." People and animals can share this disease; in fact, I have often been asked by a pediatrician to culture the throats of family pets in which a child is constantly coming down with strep throat. The diagnosis is clinched with a bacterial throat culture, which turns up positive in these cases for *streptococci* bacteria. Treatment should begin immediately when tonsillitis is suspected. Oral antibiotics in the penicillin family usually prove effective. You should start to see a dramatic improvement within the first 24–48 hours of antibiotic therapy. Because swallowing is painful for these kittens, try feeding him a liquid diet. Untreated tonsillitis often develop into bronchitis or pneumonia.

Disease Info Box

Disease	Tonsillitis (strep throat)
Common Symptoms	Swollen, red tonsils, gagging, fever, not eating
Diagnosis	Throat exam, throat culture
Treatment Options	Oral antibiotics, liquid diets

Chapter 11

Heart Diseases

People tend to think of heart disease as something to worry about as they get older. The basic idea holds true for cats, too. However, a few heart diseases occur in younger cats and kittens. Some of them are infectious diseases, one is a nutritional deficiency, one has an unknown cause, and three of them are congenital birth defects. Let's begin with the congenitals.

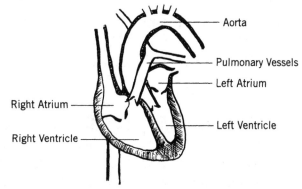

Patent Ductus Arteriosus (PDA)

PDA is a common congenital heart defect in kittens. During the development of the fetus, a duct exists between the left pulmonary artery to the aorta, causing blood to bypass the lungs because the lungs aren't functional in the fetus. At birth, this channel closes,

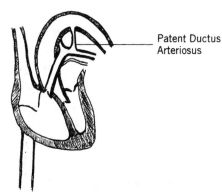

A diagram of a normal heart (top) and one of a heart with patent ductus arteriosus (bottom). This causes the lungs to flood with blood, which causes difficulty breathing.

directing the newborn's blood to the lungs so it can exchange oxygen from air. If the arterial duct (ductus arteriosus) remains open (patent), a shunting of blood occurs through the duct from the aorta to the pulmonary artery, overloading the artery and flooding the lungs with blood. The consequences are wet lungs, difficulty breathing, rapid respiratory rate, and eventually, death.

Upon examination, your veterinarian hears a very loud murmur on the left side of an affected kitten's chest wall. The left side of the heart stresses from the increased pressure in the lungs and enlarges to compensate. The aorta can even develop a bulge from the pressure (called an *aneurysm*). Diagnosis is made by an electrocardiogram and chest x-ray, which show left-sided heart enlargement. Angiography with contrast material to demonstrate the duct confirms the diagnosis. Treatment is surgical ligation (tying off) of the duct. Without doing that, the lungs become wet and the heart weakens to the point that it fails completely.

Disease Info Box

Disease	Patent ductus arteriosus
Common Symptoms	Loss of energy and breath, loud murmur
Diagnosis	Electrocardiogram, angiogram, x-ray
Treatment Options	Surgical ligation of duct

Ventricular Septal Defect (VSD)

VSD is another common congenital heart defect seen in kittens. It consists of a hole in the wall (or septa) between the left and right ventricles. Because the pressure is higher in the left ventricle than the right, blood shunts from the left ventricle to the right one. Any breed of cat can get this defect. The signs are heart failure, coughing, loss of energy, pale mucous membranes, and a loud heart murmur heard on the right side of the chest. Since electro-cardiograms and chest x-rays generally show normal, an echocardiogram (ultrasound of the heart) is the test of choice. The hole in the septa between the ventricles is easily visualized. Treatment isn't necessary if the hole is small, but some cases require surgical closure of the hole. Several post-operative complications convince most veterinarians to try to treat these cases with medical treatment rather than surgery if at all possible. Either way, many of these kittens don't do well and have to be euthanized.

Disease Info Box

Disease	Ventricular septal defect
Common Symptoms	Loss of breath, coughing, pale mucus membranes
Diagnosis	Loud murmur, heart sonogram
Treatment Options	Medical drugs, surgical closure of defect

Heart Valve Defects

The heart valves are the one-way doors in the heart that keep the blood flowing in one direction, from chamber to chamber. These valves are crucial to keeping the heart pumping efficiently. Without them, the blood would flow in two directions, back and forth in the heart chambers, causing total heart failure. Most people think of this degeneration of a heart valve as an old age change, and that's usually right. But in kittens, they are either born with defective heart valves (Siamese or Burmese), or have had a disease that causes the valves to deform and deteriorate, essentially causing a sudden, rapid aging of the heart.

The diseases that can cause degeneration of heart valves are chronic systemic infections, such as skin or dental, and certain viral infections. Whatever the cause, the kitten has sudden bouts of difficulty breathing, coughing, and possibly fainting spells. Your veterinarian can hear abnormal heart sounds, loud murmurs, and even arrhythmic heart beats. The final diagnosis is made using an ultrasound of the heart valves. They would appear thickened and malfunctioning. If an infection is suspected, systemic antibiotics are given for several weeks and the heart condition is monitored. If the condition is congenital or from a viral infection, the prognosis is worse. Ultimately, the kitten will go into heart failure if the valves do not respond to treatment.

Disease Info Box

Disease	Heart valve defect
Common Symptoms	Difficulty breathing, fainting, coughing
Diagnosis	Loud murmur, heart sonogram
Treatment Options	Treat underlying disease, heart medications

Myocarditis

Myocarditis isn't a congenital condition; it's a disease brought on by an infectious organism, like a bacteria or virus. This disease can strike at any age. Certain diseases have a potential to infect heart muscle and inner structures. One virus known to infect heart muscles is the feline panleukopenia virus. A parasitic disease that can do the same is toxoplasmosis. These diseases cause an inflammation of the heart, and can cause heart disease, heart arrhythmia, and sudden cardiac failure. The diagnosis of these cases is tricky because your vet has to determine the underlying cause. Blood tests, physical exams, ECGs, heart sonograms and other diagnostic tests are usually needed. Once your vet finds the underlying cause, he can start appropriate treatment. Besides treating the primary disease, specific heart medications can be started. Complete recovery is possible in these cases, but permanent heart damage is always possible, too.

Disease Info Box

Disease	Myocarditis
Common Symptoms	Heart arrhythmia, heart failure, fever, symptoms to 1º disease
Diagnosis	Blood tests, physical exam, heart sonogram
Treatment Options	Primary disease first, heart medications

Cardiomyopathy

Cardiomyopathy means disease of the heart muscle. It's almost identical to myocarditis, the difference being that cardiomyopathy isn't caused by an infectious disease. This section discusses the two different forms of cardio-myopathy, hypertrophic and dilated, in turn.

Hypertrophic Cardiomyopathy

Hypertrophic cardiomyopathy, a condition in which the heart muscle becomes very thickened, which reduces the size of the heart chambers and the volume of blood that it can pump. Causes vary. Certain kitten families are genetically predisposed to this disease. In older cats, an overactive thyroid gland can cause it.

These kittens go into a heart failure with coughing, loss of breath and breathing distress, pale gums, and strokes. Hypertrophic cardiomyopathy can lead to stroke. The most common stroke involves a blood clot sitting in the aorta where it splits, causing sudden paralysis of both hind legs. The aorta is the main artery that feeds the body with oxygenated blood. It splits, or bifurcates,

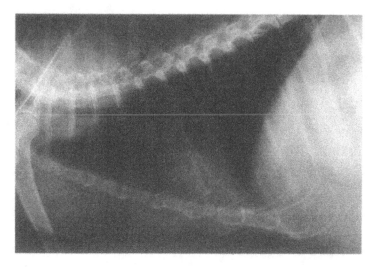

An x-ray of a kitten with cardiomyopathy, an enlarged, thickened heart.

when it gets to the hind legs. Right at that "Y," a blood clot can get caught up and stop the flow of blood to either leg. This is called a *saddle thromboembolism* and is common in hypertrophic cardiomyopathy. These kittens have fast heart rates and are paralyzed in the rear legs.

Diagnosis is best made by visualizing the enlarged and thickened heart chambers on an electrocardiogram (electric tracing of heart beat), chest x-ray, and on a cardiac sonogram. A thyroid blood test also should be done to rule out a hyperactive thyroid (*hyperthyroidism*). The vet recommends blood thinners to prevent stroke, and if the animal has an overactive thyroid, a specific medication, as well. Even with treatment, these cases will always need medication and constant veterinary supervision. I have had many cases of hypertrophic cats living full lives.

Dilated Cardiomyopathy

The dilated form is the opposite of the hypertrophic form, and is rarely seen in young kittens. The heart muscle becomes dilated and stretched, weakens, and cannot pump the blood efficiently. Certain breeds—Siamese, Abyssinian and Burmese—are predisposed. A fairly new cause that has been identified is a lack of taurine amino acid in the diet. Most commercial cat foods now add taurine to their cat foods, dramatically reducing the incidence of this disease. Symptoms are similar to the hypertrophic form: coughing, breathing distress, pale gums, arrhythmic heart beats, and sudden death.

Diagnosis is best made by visualizing the enlarged and thickened heart chambers on an electrocardiogram (electric tracing of heart beat), chest x-ray and on cardiac sonogram. The ideal treatment uses cardiac drugs and taurine supplements. Certain drugs are available for treating this disease, but the prognosis is poor.

Disease Info Box

Disease	Cardiomyopathy
Common Symptoms	Heart arrhythmia, heart failure, breathing distress, coughing, pale gums
Diagnosis	Electrocardiogram, cardiac sonogram, chest x-ray
Treatment Options	Cardiac drugs, Taurine supplements, blood thinners, anti-thyroid medication when needed (in Hypertrophic form)

Feline Heartworm

Veterinarians used to think heartworm was particular to dogs, but have since learned that cats can get it, too. Heartworm is a parasite named *Dirofilaria immitis*, which is much like the roundworms described in Chapter 2, but which inhabits the heart and lung blood vessels rather than the intestine. The disease spreads through infected mosquitoes, which inject the infective larvae of the worm into the kitten when they bite. From there, the larva migrates until it ends up in the chambers of the heart and blood vessels of the lungs. It matures into an adult and multiplies.

Symptoms usually include coughing several months after being bitten, and progress to pale mucus membranes, lethargy, and breathing distress. Diagnosis is made through a very sensitive blood test called an *antigen* test, which detects the presence of the worm in the blood stream. Chest x-rays show an enlarged heart and thickened lung blood vessels. An ultrasound might actually visualize the worms living in the heart chambers. Treatment is imprecise, since all the drugs used to treat heartworm are canine drugs.

Disease Info Box

Disease	Feline heartworm
Common Symptoms	Coughing, breathing distress, lung embolism
Diagnosis	Electrocardiogram, cardiac sonogram, chest x-ray
Treatment Options	Canine approved arsenic-based drugs (use with caution in kittens)

Chapter 12

Respiratory Problems

K ittens are particularly susceptible to respiratory ailments. I see many kittens with sneezing, coughing, and runny eyes and nose. Most of the ailments are infectious diseases, but a few are parasitic or internal conditions. This chapter is a little longer than the last few, but it's very important. It starts with upper respiratory diseases and ends with lower respiratory ones. The respiratory tract runs from the nose, sinus, and windpipe (upper respiratory), to the bronchi and lungs (lower respiratory tract).

Viral Upper Respiratory Infection (URI)

 An URI is an infection of the upper respiratory tract, which includes the nares (nostrils), sinuses, throat, larynx (voice box), and trachea (windpipe). The most common causes of URI in kittens are viruses, usually feline rhinotracheitis virus and calicivirus (for a complete discussion, see chapter 2). These viruses easily invade the kitten's respiratory tract through the eyes and nose and cause sneezing, coughing, watery and clear running red eyes and nose, fever, and swollen neck glands.

These infections are very contagious through the bodily fluids like the sneeze fluid droplets that spew out of a kitten's nose during a sneeze.

Diagnosis is easy for an experienced veterinarian. Treatment begins with oral antibiotics and antibiotic ophthalmic drops. Nasal decongestants can help dry up the nasal passages, which can prove very important—if a cat can't smell his food, he doesn't eat it. Most of these kittens aren't eating because of their stuffed up nose. Using steam vaporizers or five minutes in a steamy bathroom can loosen up nasal congestion and help the kitten

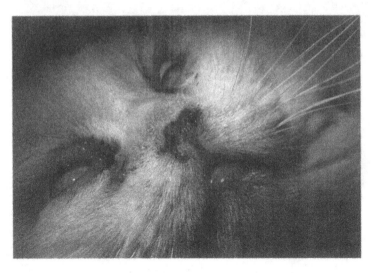

This kitten has an upper respiratory infection that's causing runny nose and eyes.

breathe. Keep these kittens away from other cats because these viruses are highly contagious. The best way to prevent them in the first place is to vaccinate all kittens according to the vaccine schedule detailed in Chapter 2.

Disease Info Box

Disease	Viral upper respiratory infection
Common Symptoms	Sneezing, runny red eyes, coughing, fever, clear nasal discharge
Diagnosis	Clinical symptoms, clear nasal and eye discharge
Treatment Options	Oral and ophthalmic antibiotics, steam, decongestants

Bacterial URI

The bacterial form of URI, also known as *pneumonitis*, usually is caused by the bacteria *chlamydia psittaci*. Other bacteria commonly infect the respiratory tracts of kittens, such as *mycoplasma* and *streptococcus* strains. The symptoms and diagnosis are similar to viral URI, with two differences: the eye and nasal discharge in bacterial infections isn't clear like in viral—it's thick and yellow or green—and the veterinarian can run bacterial cultures to identify the agent. Treatment includes appropriate oral and ophthalmic antibiotics, as well as decongestants and steam therapy (five minutes in a steamy bathroom, or a steam vaporizer). Bacterial URIs are contagious to other cats, so isolate your infected kittens.

Disease Info Box

Disease	Bacterial upper respiratory infection
Common Symptoms	Sneezing, runny red eyes, coughing, fever, thick nasal discharge
Diagnosis	Clinical symptoms, bacterial culture
Treatment Options	Oral and ophthalmic antibiotics, steam, decongestants

Sinusitis

Sinusitis is the inflammation of the lining of the sinuses. Many people suffer from sinusitis. In kittens, it's usually a sequel to URI. In healthy kittens, URI viruses don't stay around for long. The bacteria tend to colonize the lining of the sinuses as well as the nasal passages, and getting rid of them thereafter can prove rather difficult. These kittens are sickly, with chronic sneezing, thick nasal discharge, coughing owing to a postnasal drip, fever, sinus pressure and pain, bloody noses especially with sneezing, and loss of appetite.

The diagnosis is important because your veterinarian must differentiate between just a URI and sinusitis. A sinus x-ray or endoscopic exam can help make the call. A bacterial culture will help identify the bacteria and find the appropriate antibiotic for treatment. Treatment entails long-term antibiotics, decongestants, steam therapy (five minutes in a steamy bathroom, or a steam vaporizer). If your kitten has chronic sinusitis that lasts longer than two weeks, your veterinarian should run a feline leukemia and feline immunodeficiency virus test.

Disease Info Box

Disease	Sinusitis
Common Symptoms	Thick yellow nasal discharge, sneezing, nosebleeds, fever
Diagnosis	Clinical symptoms, bacterial culture, sinus x-ray, endoscopic exam, FeLV-FIV test
Treatment Options	Long term oral antibiotics, steam therapy, decongestants

Nosebleeds

Several concern-worthy factors can cause nosebleeds in kittens. If your kitten has frequent nosebleeds, meaning at least one per month, you might want your veterinarian to go through this checklist looking for the cause.

Checklist for Kitten Nosebleeds

- Excessive sneezing from upper respiratory infections
- Bleeding disorders or hemophilia
- Sinusitis
- Sinus tumors
- Nasal trauma

The different causes of nosebleeds usually can be differentiated by performing a few diagnostic tests, such as a sinus exam, sinus bacterial culture, blood tests for blood clotting disorders or hemophilia, sinus and nasal x-rays, sinus endoscopy to visualize sinus lining, or feline leukemia virus and feline immunodeficiency virus blood tests.

Treating nosebleeds can be simple or complicated. Some techniques used to stop nosebleeds are as follows:

- Raise nose upward to slow blood flow to nose
- Place ice packs on bridge of nose to slow nose bleed
- Keep kitten calm by wrapping in towel to keep blood pressure down
- Spray nasal decongestant sprays or drops that contain *epinephrine* up the nostril—these products constrict blood vessels in the nose and slow bleeding

Disease Info Box

Disease	Nosebleeds
Common Symptoms	Bloody nose, especially with sneezing
Diagnosis	Clinical symptoms, sinus x-ray, sinus endoscopy, bacterial culture, FeLV and FIV testing
Treatment Options	Elevate nose, ice packs, calm kitten, nasal decongestants

Bronchitis

The bronchi are the main breathing tubes that run into each lung. These tubes must stay open and patent for the air to freely flow in and out of the lungs with each breath. Anything that affects these airways affects normal breathing. *Bronchitis* is the inflammation of the bronchial tubes. This inflammation can take the form of an infection, viral or bacterial, or a reaction to a caustic substance like chemical fumes, smoke, or extremely cold air.

In kittens, most cases of bronchitis that veterinarians see are infectious. Most of them are a continuation of an untreated URI or one that hasn't responded to treatment. Viruses like feline rhinotracheitis, feline calicivirus, feline leukemia, and feline immunodeficiency virus can find their way into the bronchi.

Examples of bacteria that can infect bronchial tubes are *streptococcus, pasturella, chlamydia (pneumonitis)*, and *mycoplasma*. A bacterial culture can identify which bacteria is the causative agent. These bacteria cause the bronchial walls to become inflamed, thickened, and wet with mucus or pus secretions, leading to fever, coughing, and breathing distress. These kittens are seriously ill, at risk of dying. They should not be stressed in any way because they're already not getting enough air owing to the constricted airways. The diagnosis is made by listening to the wheezing sounds of the lungs with a stethoscope, and visualizing the thickened bronchi on a chest x-ray.

Treatment should commence immediately upon diagnosis. Broad spectrum antibiotics appropriate for the specific bacteria are crucial for treatment. Certain drugs, called *bronchodilators*, can open the constricted bronchi, such as *aminophylline*, which helps the kitten breath easier. Cough suppressants and expectorants help with the cough. In severe cases, using oxygen support can allow the kitten to breath easier by getting a higher oxygen saturation in a smaller volume of air. Many of these kittens aren't eating, often requiring nutritional support.

Disease Info Box

Disease	Bronchitis
Common Symptoms	Persistent cough, fever, breathing distress, loss of appetite
Diagnosis	Increased lung sounds, bacterial culture, chest x-ray
Treatment Options	Long term oral antibiotics, bronchodilator (Aminophylline), cough suppressants, expectorants, supportive care

Pneumonia

Anything that interferes with the exchange of oxygen and carbon dioxide in the lungs affects breathing. The same causes of bronchitis can cause pneumonia.

Viral pneumonia and bacterial pneumonia are common in young kittens (see the section on bronchitis for specific causes). The symptoms are similar: coughing and wheezing, breathing distress, fever, loss of appetite and weight loss. When bronchitis and pneumonia occur together, as they often do, it's called *bronchopneumonia*. Your veterinarian can differentiate between bronchitis and pneumonia on a chest x-ray. The pattern is different and can tell your vet where the disease is, how severe it is, and what the prognosis is. Treatment is similar to bronchitis. The prognosis for cases of pneumonia is a bit worse than for bronchitis.

Disease Info Box	
Disease	Pneumonia
Common Symptoms	Persistent cough, fever, breathing distress, loss of appetitie
Diagnosis	Increased lung sounds heard on exam, bacterial culture, chest x-ray
Treatment Options	Long term oral antibiotics, bronchodilators cough suppressants, expectorants, supportive care

Pleuritis

Other words for *pleuritis* are *pleurisy* and *pleural effusion*. Pleuritis is an inflammation of the pleura, which is the inner lining of the chest cavity. Most kittens with pleuritis have it for one of two reasons: they sustained a penetrating wound to the chest (like a bite wound from another animal), which introduced bacteria into the chest cavity and caused a bacterial infection, or the feline infectious peritonitis (FIP) virus infected the pleura.

Chapter 2 includes a complete discussion of FIP which causes inflammation of many organs and within the chest and abdomen, usually involving fluid accumulation, fever, weight loss, breathing distress, coughing, and often the kitten's demise.

The bacterial form is easier to treat. The bacteria often infect the lungs and produce a secondary pneumonia. Fluid accumulates in the chest, causing difficulty breathing and possibly leading to heart failure. Diagnosis uses blood tests for FIP and bacterial cultures of the chest fluid. X-rays show the fluid settling in the chest, obscuring the heart silhouette. This fluid often needs to be drained with a needle to allow easier breathing.

These cases can be critical and require immediate attention. Unfortunately, kittens who have FIP have many hurdles to overcome. Treatment is the same for pneumonia, plus the fluid is drained from the chest.

Disease Info Box	
Disease	Pleuritis
Common Symptoms	Persistent cough, fever, breathing distress, loss of appetite
Diagnosis	Muffled heart sounds, bacterial culture, FIP test, chest x-ray
Treatment Options	Long term oral antibiotics, chest tap to drain fluid

Feline Asthma

Asthma is a condition where the bronchi of the lungs constrict, narrowing the amount of air that can be inhaled. Asthmatics have breathing distress and wheezing on inhaling. The airway constriction can be so severe that it can be life threatening. These attacks are usually sudden and can come on at any time. Most asthmatic attacks can be traced to an allergic reaction to something in the kitten's environment.

These allergies can be triggered by different sources:

- **Inhalant substances:** Pollen, dust, smoke, chemical fumes, mold spores, carpeting, trees, grasses, dusty kitty litter
- **Food allergies:** Chicken, beef, dairy foods, corn, wheat, soybean, seafood
- **Contact allergies:** Wool, cotton, kapok, insecticides

Exactly what your kitten is allergic to can be determined by an allergy RAST blood test. The allergic reaction in asthmatic cats causes a sudden constriction of the muscles that line the walls of the bronchi. In addition to the constriction, a mucus secretion also further narrows the bronchial tubes. Coughing, wheezing, open mouth breathing, sitting up versus lying down to ease breathing, loss of appetite, and blue mucus membranes are all symptoms.

Your vet can diagnose asthma by hearing the wheezing sounds with a stethoscope and seeing a typical bronchial pattern on a chest x-ray. Your veterinarian has to rule out other causes of wheezing and coughing, such as bronchitis and pneumonia.

Treatment is started immediately with drugs that stop the allergic reaction, such as cortisone medication and bronchodilators that open up the constricted bronchi. Oxygen therapy might be needed to ease the breathing distress. Antihistamine drugs, however, *do not* work the same wonders in cats as they do in people.

I have, in severe cases, used human pocket inhaler bronchodilators in an asthma attack in cats. How? Roll up a piece of paper so it makes a funnel or megaphone. Place the large end over the face of the kitten, and pump the inhaler into the small end so the mist of the inhaler is inside the rolled paper. Your kitten has no choice but to breathe the air with the medicine dispersed in it. I have had my clients tell me that this technique has saved their cat's life on more than one occasion.

After you know what your kitten is allergic to, you can take steps to remove those things from his environment or diet. You might need to remove wool rugs, clean all the dust in the house, change to a dustless kitty litter, or place him on a special diet.

If your kitten doesn't respond to the medication, or you object to having him on it all the time and cannot eliminate things by changing diet, removing things from your home, cleaning dust and mold, or running air purifiers, then you might want to try desensitizing him to his allergies. Desensitizing means you are making him less allergic to these things, and the process uses allergy shots custom-designed specifically to your kitten's allergies. Small doses are given at regular intervals, usually weekly to start. The dose is increased slightly each time to gradually desensitize your kitten. The process has to be slow so that the shot doesn't actually cause an asthma attack.

Using a bronchodilator with a funnel to administer asthma medicine to a kitten.

It takes several months of weekly shots before you can expect improvement. Eventually, these shots can be spread out to biweekly and then monthly. You can never really just stop, because your kitten could become sensitized again. This is the only true cure for allergies. It takes a true commitment in time and finances to go this route, but if you have an asthmatic kitten, it might be the best solution.

Lungworms (Aelurostongylus)

Lungworms are a parasite of cats that live in the lungs. The name of the worm is *aelurostongylus*. The lifecycle of the lungworm is complicated because it has two intermediate hosts. This means that the lungworm needs two other animals other than the cat to complete its lifecycle. Here's how it goes:

The lungworm eggs pass out in the feces of the infected cat. The eggs hatch into larvae (immature worms), which snails then eat. Rodents then eat the snails and the larvae continue to live in the rodent tissues. The cat then eats the rodent and becomes infected with the larvae.

Once inside the cat, the larvae journey to the lungs and generate some mild tissue disruption. The symptoms are mild respiratory problems and coughing. A veterinarian can diagnose lungworms in two ways: a fecal sample exam will show the eggs of the lungworms and an x-ray will show the lung tissue reaction to the worms in the lungs. Treatment is simple, using worming (anthelmintic) medications.

Thoracic Lymphosarcoma

Thoracic lymphosarcoma is a form of cancer that occurs in the chest of cats. In kittens, lymphosarcoma cancer can occur if the kitten has the viral disease feline leukemia. After a kitten gets the leukemia virus, the virus can spread throughout the body's organ systems and cause lymphosarcoma cancer, an aggressive malignant cancer that quickly spreads to many internal organs. One of the common sites is in the membrane that separates the left from right sides of the chest cavity.

As the tumor grows, it takes up space in the chest, rendering breathing increasingly difficult. Considerable fluid often builds up from the tumor. Your veterinarian can readily diagnose these tumors from a chest x-ray, which outlines the tumor in the middle of the chest, as well as the fluid in the chest cavity. A feline leukemia blood test must be done. After a positive result is confirmed, the diagnosis of thoracic lymphosarcoma can be made. These tumors are extremely difficult to remove surgically, and chemotherapy has only limited success. Most of these kittens die from these tumors or other viral induced complications.

Disease Info Box

Disease	Thoracic lymphosarcoma
Common Symptoms	Coughing, breathing difficulties, fluid in chest cavity
Diagnosis	Chest x-ray, FeLV test
Treatment Options	Limited supportive care, chemotherapy

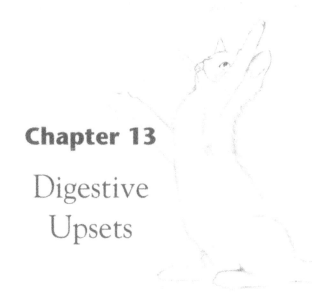

Chapter 13

Digestive
Upsets

K ittens can contract a wide variety of digestive upsets, ranging from
vomiting to diarrhea and plenty in-between. This chapter starts out
with the things that upset little kitty stomachs, then moves on to the
intestines, and ends with colon disturbances and miscellaneous ones. The
way to use this chapter is to look under the topic for what's ailing your kitten.
Then look for the ailment that fits your kitten's problem. The main thing to
remember here is that many digestive upsets have the same symptoms but
different causes. Your veterinarian should be able to distinguish between
them.

Gastritis and Vomiting

Kittens are highly prone to vomiting and stomach problems. Kittens can feel
sick to their stomach for many reasons. Don't be alarmed if your kitten
vomits just once. It happens. When he vomits two or more times in one day,
or once several days in a row, now you want give your vet a call. *Gastritis*
means inflammation of the stomach. It often leads to vomiting. The actual
act of *vomiting* is when the stomach contracts, forcing out food, fluids, and
other contents (bile, white foam, acid, foreign materials). When kittens are
nauseous, they often drool copiously and swallow frequently.

When kittens have an upset stomach, they do several things that you
might notice. First, they stop eating. Then they stretch out their neck and
might make gagging or coughing sounds. In severe cases, your kitten's
abdomen heaves and wretches, sometimes violently during vomiting.

Many different things can cause a kitten to be nauseous, including some
of the more common ones listed here:

- Acute kidney failure (as seen in antifreeze toxicity)
- Certain intestinal inflammatory diseases
- Certain medications
- Constipation (severe)
- Eating foreign materials
- Fever
- Food poisoning
- Gastroenteritis (infectious, foreign bodies)
- Hairballs
- Internal parasites (esp. Roundworms)
- Intestinal obstruction
- Pancreatitis
- Stomach lymphosarcoma cancer
- Stomach ulcers
- Toxins
- Viral gastroenteritis (feline panleukopenia and corona viruses)

Relieving Digestive Upsets

- Withhold food for 12–24 hours from the onset of vomiting.
- Give only several ounces of water at a time, or ice cubes in a bowl so that he can't drink too much too fast.
- Check to see if he also has diarrhea—this can be a clue of the cause.
- Bring a stool sample to your veterinarian to check for internal parasites.
- Check for any toxic substance, spoiled food, or foreign substance your kitten might have ingested.
- Ask family members if anyone gave him any medication.
- Check for fever or symptoms of other diseases.
- If you see blood in the vomit, call your veterinarian immediately.

Your vet does a physical exam looking for clues to the vomiting, checking for pain in the abdomen, loud intestinal sounds, fever, pale mucus membranes, and stomach bloating.

Regurgitation

Regurgitation differs from vomiting in two ways: the food substances are not digested and the stomach doesn't contract. Food substances swallowed too fast come right back up before they even make it to the stomach. The food that comes up looks just the same as it went down, and doesn't include vomit odor or bile. The three most common causes of regurgitation in kittens are hairballs, eating or drinking too fast, and *megaesophagus*, a congenital defect of the esophagus that causes it to dilate so it cannot transport food from the mouth to the stomach

Your veterinarian diagnoses these cases by ruling out each disorder. For instance, hairballs can be diagnosed on an x-ray and be treated with laxatives. If your kitten eats too quickly, you might have to change how you feed him—small meals several times a day are better than one or two large meals. Megaesophagus is very difficult to treat and usually involve feeding liquid diets from a raised position. Your vet will go over several different treatment options.

Hairballs

Hairballs are one of the most common stomach ailments from which cats suffer. Owing to a cat's fastidious grooming habits, many lick and swallow much of their own hair—especially long-haired cats. The hair often sits in the stomach, where it forms a clump or ball, which can cause nausea, vomiting, regurgitation, weight loss, and stomach bloating. These symptoms can persist for weeks before the kitten stops eating entirely. Diagnosis is made by means of an x-ray, where shadows of the hair can often be seen. Treatment can be as simple as giving a dose of mineral oil, which lubricates the hair and helps it either pass out in the stool or come up in vomit. Other laxatives come in a tube and are available over-the-counter. They work better as a preventive than a treatment. All long-haired cats should get a prophylactic dose of these laxatives in a tube once or twice a week to help prevent hairballs. In severe cases, the hairball needs to be surgically removed if it's causing an intestinal obstruction.

Disease Info Box	
Disease	Hairball
Common Symptoms	Excessive drooling, vomiting, gagging, coughing
Diagnosis	Physical exam, x-ray, upper GI series, endoscopy
Treatment Options	Laxatives, surgical removal of hairball

Pancreatitis

Pancreatitis is inflammation of the *pancreas gland*. The pancreas serves several essential purposes: it produces the insulin hormone, which is crucial for maintaining blood sugar levels, and it produces enzymes necessary for digestion. In pancreatitis, the gland malfunctions and leaks these digestive enzymes into the abdomen, causing sudden and severe vomiting, fever, abdominal pain, and bloating. Pancreatitis is most often seen in overweight cats who eat high fat diets. A diagnosis can be made via a blood test. Two such tests that can check pancreatic function are *amylase* and *lipase*. If these test numbers are greatly elevated, it suggests inflammation of the pancreas. This disease can be very severe and can require hospitalization, supportive care, antibiotics, and intravenous fluids and nutrition. Weight loss and low fat diets might be in order.

Enteritis

Enteritis is defined as inflammation of the intestines. The intestines of cats are comprised of two sections: the small intestine (duodenum, jejunum, and

Disease Info Box

Disease	Pancreatitis
Common Symptoms	Excessive drooling, vomiting, gagging, fever, abdominal pain
Diagnosis	Physical exam, x-ray, blood tests
Treatment Options	Supportive care, IV fluids, antibiotics, low fat diets

ileum), and large intestine (colon and rectum). The small intestine is where food and nutrients are absorbed and the large intestine is where water is absorbed. If the intestines aren't functioning properly, digestion becomes difficult, leading to abdominal bloating, cramping, diarrhea, and vomiting.

Many things can cause enteritis—basically anything that causes inflammation of the intestines. Below are some of the most common causes seen in kittens.

Viral Enteritis

Two common viruses cause enteritis in cats: feline panleukopenia virus and feline coronavirus. Panleukopenia is a virus very similar to the *parvovirus* of dogs. Young kittens are most susceptible and get this virus through oral contamination with bodily fluids of an infected cat. Symptoms can occur quickly, within a day or so, and are high fever (above 103°F), brain damage with neurological problems, vomiting and mucus yellow diarrhea, dehydration, and a pronounced reduction of disease fighting white blood cells (WBC). The intestines are bloated and possibly nonfunctional. There can be vomiting and profuse watery (usually yellow) diarrhea.

Treatment aims to correct the dehydration and prevent secondary infections due to the low WBC count. Antibiotics, electrolyte fluids, and nutritional/vitamin supplements are given aggressively. Treatment for the diarrhea is covered later in this chapter. Many of these kittens die within several days, making the prognosis poor. The best prevention is having your kitten inoculated against the virus (see Chapter 2, "First Visit to the Veterinarian's).

Coronavirus enteritis isn't as serious and many owners don't even know their kitten has it. The intestinal form of coronavirus is related to the feline infectious peritonitis (FIP) virus. Luckily, the enteric form doesn't cause any of the FIP disease. The symptoms are mild diarrhea that persists for only a few days. Usually, the vet simply needs to symptomatically treat for diarrhea (covered later in the chapter).

Food Poisoning (Salmonella)

Kittens love to chase and pounce on moving objects to practice their hunting skills, which can be fun to watch, but often leads to actual hunting behavior as he gets to three or four months of age. The one problem with this is natural habit it that the kitten can catch diseases from killing or eating rodents and insects—toxoplasmosis and lungworms are two of numerous possibilities already discussed. Bacterial infection of the intestines is another. One such bacteria is *salmonella*, which causes *salmonellosis*.

Cats become infected by hunting birds, eating spoiled food, or contact with the infected feces of an infected animal. One way or the other, ingesting the bacteria by mouth gets the ball rolling. Once the salmonella moves in, it causes inflammation of the intestinal lining, leading to severe gastro-enteritis—vomiting, diarrhea, fever, abdominal bloating and cramps, malnutrition, and dehydration. These kittens often have bloody diarrhea. The diagnosis is made by a bacterial culture of the feces.

I treat these cases aggressively with replacement electrolyte fluids, anti-biotics, bland diets (chicken/rice/yogurt) and anti-diarrhea medications (see *diarrhea* later in this chapter). Some of these kittens require hospitalization. Because salmonella can infect people, you need to wash your hands after you handle the litter box and disinfect all food and water bowls as well as the litter box several times daily. Consult your doctor for your health concerns.

Eosinophilic Enteritis

Eosinophilic enteritis is a strange disease in which the lining of the intestines become infiltrated and thickened with a particular type of white blood cell called *eosinophils*. The infiltration can be quite extensive throughout the intestines, disrupting their functioning and leading to digestive problems. The cause is unknown, although some think it's triggered by an allergic reaction to the cat food. These kittens can become debilitated and undernourished to the point of emaciation. Cases are usually diagnosed by a biopsy of the intestine lining. Treatment is difficult and usually consists of dietary changes to bland foods, and cortisone medications to reduce the intestinal thickening.

Disease Info Box

Disease	Enteritis
Common Symptoms	Chronic digestive disorders, diarrhea, emaciation
Diagnosis	Biopsy of intestinal lining
Treatment Options	Bland diet, cortisone mediations

Intestinal Obstruction

Kittens, more than most animals, are very curious creatures, which causes them to put all sorts of things into their mouths, such as the following:

- Ribbons
- Rubber bands
- Pieces of string
- Dental floss
- Tinsel from Christmas trees

A cat's tongue is bristled for grooming, but these bristles also create a one-way flow of hair and objects. In other words, cats basically must swallow what they get in their mouths, which inevitably leads to problems. If kittens get string or a *linear foreign body* in their mouths, they usually swallow it. Linear foreign bodies are very difficult to pass through the intestines. What usually happens is that they get caught in the stomach or small intestines.

The symptoms of a linear foreign body are:

- Loss of appetite
- Sudden vomiting
- Abdominal pain and bloating
- String wrapped around the base of the tongue or coming out the rectum

You should bring your kitten to the veterinarian immediately if you note any of these symptoms, or if you see the string in the mouth. Your vet takes an x-ray and could see a classic "pleating" pattern, which happens when the string tries to pass through the intestines. Some of these cases require an upper GI series, in which the patient drinks barium prior to the x-rays, highlighting the string on film.

Endoscopy is another tool used to visualize the inside of the digestive tract. An endoscope is a long, fiber-optic tool that has a lens and light at the tip. It's inserted down the esophagus into the stomach and upper small intestines under general anesthesia, giving your veterinarian a good look at what is in there. Most endoscopes also have a feature that allows the operator to grasp the string in an attempt to remove it. Sometimes none of these measures work and your vet might recommend exploratory surgery.

Disease Info Box

Disease	Intestinal obstruction
Common Symptoms	Sudden loss of appetite & vomiting, abdominal pain
Diagnosis	X-ray, upper GI series, endoscopy, surgery
Treatment Options	Endoscopy, laxatives, surgical removal of string

Diarrhea and Colitis

Everybody has had *diarrhea*, but few people know what causes it. Let me explain. As food substances pass through the small intestine, nutrients are absorbed. When it enters the large intestine, most of which is called the *colon*, it becomes *stool*, and water must be absorbed. The colon is where water is absorbed out of the stool. If the stool passes through the colon too quickly, the colon doesn't have a chance to absorb the water and the stool expresses in a diarrhea mode. The animal feels the urgency of the wet stool in the colon and rectum and defecates.

Colitis is inflammation of the large intestine, or colon. Severe and persistent cases of diarrhea generally are considered to be colitis. You often see bloody diarrhea in colitis. Many things can cause diarrhea and colitis in kittens, including some of the most common reasons in the following list:

- Overeating
- Sudden change in diet
- Eating a diet that is too "rich" or high fat content
- Internal parasites
- Lactose intolerance (see Chapter 4, "Feeding and Nutrition")
- Viral diseases—Feline Panleukopenia virus and Coronavirus
- Food poisoning—salmonellosis
- Inflammatory bowel disease (IBD)

The degree of diarrhea can vary with the cause. In a case of sudden dietary change, for example, the stool might be soft, but in a case of internal parasites, or viral diseases, the stool can be watery. The diagnosis depends on the disease, but usually involves a fecal exam, physical exam, and perhaps even an abdominal x-ray.

The treatment of diarrhea does depend on the cause, but a few common treatments can help most cases of diarrhea. The main thrust is two-fold:

correct the fluid loss and dehydration to make up for the fluid loss during diarrhea and slow down the bowels.

Treating Diarrhea

- Feed bland foods of jarred chicken baby food and rice rather than kitten food
- Give one-half teaspoon of Kaopectate orally twice daily to slow the bowels down
- Add water, or chicken broth, to the chicken and rice mixture
- Give one teaspoon of plain yogurt with each meal
- Give extra fluids that will correct dehydration which the kitten may like, such as skim milk
- Add pediatric electrolyte solution available in pharmacies to kitten's water in a 50/50 mixture

Inflammatory bowel disease (IBD)

IBD is a severe and persistent case of colitis. The colon becomes inflamed to the point that it can no longer do its job. It cannot absorb water, and it sometimes ulcerates and bleeds. These cats have severe bloody diarrhea and abdominal bloating and cramping, and can have loss of appetite and fever. A diagnosis usually involves a biopsy of the colon, using an endoscope and its biopsy forceps. Other causes of diarrhea must be ruled out, which can require fecal exams and blood tests. Treatment is needed with replacement fluids (these kittens usually are dehydrated from all the fluid loss), antibiotics, and anti-spasmodic drugs that slows down the bowel. Dietary changes also might be called upon to manage this disease.

Disease Info Box

Disease	Diarrhea and colitis
Common Symptoms	Loose, watery and bloody stools
Diagnosis	X-ray, endoscopy, fecal exam, blood tests
Treatment Options	Dietary changes, antispasmodic drugs, antibiotics

Constipation

Constipation is the opposite of diarrhea. In constipation, the stool moves too slowly through the colon, allowing the colon to absorb too much water and leading to a hard dry stool that can prove difficult and painful to pass. You will see your kitten straining in the litter box without passing stool. Constipation usually involves abdominal cramps and loss of appetite, and in severe cases, sometimes even vomiting. Seek veterinary advice.

The causes of constipation vary. Some of the most common are:

- Blockage of stool due to matting of hair and feces
- Changing litter box placement in house, or brand of litter can lead to a kitten avoiding the box
- Congenital enlargement of the colon called *Megacolon* seen in Siamese cats where the stool is retained and impacts so it cannot empty
- Dehydration from fever, disease, water deprivation, or inappetence
- General anesthesia and surgery
- Hemorrhoids causing pain on defecation
- Injury, trauma, or infection of rectum or anus
- Internal parasites
- Low fiber diets

Treatment for constipation really depends on the cause. Some standard treatments can help. The first are laxatives. Laxatives are medications that are not digested, so when taken orally, they reach the colon intact. There, they lubricate the hardened stool and help the body evacuate it. Mineral oil is very good for this purpose, usually between ½–1 teaspoon, given orally.

The other laxatives commercially available in a tube and commonly used to treat hairballs also can help with constipation. As another treatment option, consider using high fiber foods to keep the bowels moving. Fiber only works in the company of water, however, so you need to add water to your kitten's food before the fiber can do its job.

Disease Info Box

Disease	Constipation
Common Symptoms	Straining to defecate, hard, dry stools
Diagnosis	X-ray, endoscopy, fecal exam, blood tests
Treatment Options	Oral laxatives, suppositories, enemas, high fiber diets

Chapter 14

Liver
Diseases

Luckily, most veterinarians don't see too many liver problems in kittens, but when we do, they're usually serious. Some of the liver diseases involve the gallbladder rather than the liver itself. So that you can understand more about these diseases, let me give you a brief anatomy lesson.

The liver is a large organ that sits just behind the stomach. It has four lobes and a gallbladder, which stores bile, a thick green liquid that flows into the small intestine during digestion to digest fats. The liver has several functions, including:

- Detoxifying drugs
- Digesting fats
- Secreting and recycling bile
- Regulating energy sources
- Helping regulate blood sugar
- Manufacturing certain vitamins and hormones
- Filtering the blood
- Helping to maintain red blood cell count
- Blood clotting

Many blood vessels carry blood from the digestive tract through the liver (called *hepatic arteries* and *portal veins*), and from the liver to the heart through the *hepatic vein*. Certain ducts, or tubes, called *bile ducts*, carry the bile in the gallbladder to the small intestine during digestion. In cats, some tubes even run from the bile ducts to the pancreas.

Now you can appreciate how sick your kitten would get if its liver didn't work. Kittens can get a variety of diseases of the liver or gallbladder—some are infectious, others are birth defects. This chapter goes through each one. This is a complicated chapter, but if your kitten has one of these problems, it is well worth your effort to try to read and understand the section.

Gallbladder Disease

Three common diseases or abnormalities affect the gallbladders of kittens. Remember, the gallbladder is the storage sac for bile, which is that thick, green liquid that flows into the small intestine during a meal to digest fats. If something disrupts the flow of bile, a few common symptoms often are seen:

- Bile backs up in the gallbladder, then in the liver, and eventually in the bloodstream, causing a yellowing of the skin, called *jaundice*.
- If insufficient bile flows into the small intestine, indigestion of fats with bloating and abdominal pain (referred to as a "gall attack") results

The following sections describe the three diseases of the gallbladder.

Congenital Malformed Gallbladder

You see congenital malformed gallbladder when the gallbladder doesn't form correctly during fetal growth. As long as the outflow bile duct is patent and bile can flow into the small intestines, you won't notice any of the undesirable symptoms. These cases are diagnosed incidentally on an ultrasound or during an abdominal surgery. Few of these cases require treatment.

Gallstones

Occasionally, cats can develop stones in their gallbladder. If any of these stones block the outflow of bile, sudden pain, bloating, and abdominal discomfort directly related to eating a fatty meal (which accurately describes most cat foods) can result. You might see vomiting, fever, and a yellowing of the skin, called *jaundice*. These stones can take the form of actual pea-sized stones or of sandy, sludge-like sediment. These gallstones can be seen either on an x-ray or an ultrasound of the liver. Low-fat diets are started immediately, and surgical removal of the stones might be needed in severe or persistent cases.

Gallbladder Inflammation (Cholecystitis)

Inflammation of the gallbladder can be seen associated with gallstones, or in cases of infection, trauma (like being hit by a car), or cancer. The symptoms are the same as for gallstones. The diagnosis usually is made by an ultrasound of the liver and gallbladder and blood tests that demonstrate the increased bile in the blood and jaundice. Anti-inflammatory drugs, such as cortisone, can reduce the swelling of the gallbladder. Surgery is often needed for a gallbladder biopsy.

Disease Info Box	
Disease	Gallbladder disease
Common Symptoms	Vomiting, bloating, abdominal pain, fever
Diagnosis	X-ray, abdominal ultrasound, blood tests, biopsy
Treatment Options	Low fat diets, antiflammatory drugs

Liver Disease

Several diseases also affect the livers of young kittens. Some of them are birth defects, others are infectious diseases. This section includes a brief overview of each condition that affects kittens' livers. It is imperative that you get an early and accurate diagnosis from your veterinarian.

Hepatitis

Hepatitis is inflammation of the liver itself. Many things can cause an inflamed liver, including some the common ones in the following list:

- Bacterial infections or abscesses such as toxoplasmosis
- Drugs like Tylenol
- Toxic substances like rat poison or ammonia
- Viral diseases like feline leukemia or feline infectious peritonitis

The symptoms of hepatitis are an enlarged painful liver; yellowing of the eyes and mucus membranes, called *jaundice*; fever; elevated white blood cell counts; and elevated liver enzyme blood tests. Another blood test quite specific for liver function is called a *Bile Acid* test. The test is run first with the patient fasting and then again after the patient consumes a meal. The two results are compared to normal values. Elevated values strongly implicate liver failure. At this point, many veterinarians recommend an abdominal ultrasound to visualize the liver and gallbladder, or a liver biopsy. Often, a liver biopsy is performed under the guidance of an ultrasound with a biopsy needle.

Treatment of hepatitis usually involves antibiotics and anti-inflammatory drugs like cortisone. If the cause is a virus, your can't do much more than offer supportive care. Cases of infectious hepatitis are difficult to treat and carry a guarded to poor prognosis. In cases of poisoning and toxicosis, the prognosis varies according to the exposure.

Neonatal Jaundice

Neonatal jaundice is a condition in which kittens turn yellow, or jaundice, shortly after birth. The usual reason for this is a condition called *neonatal isoerythrolysis*. In these cases, the mother queen has antibodies to her fetus' red blood cells in her milk. When the kittens nurse, they get these antibodies, which then start to destroy their red blood cells, causing the jaundice. These kittens get anemic quite quickly. The best thing you can do is remove the kitten from the queen and start bottlefeeding it. Call your veterinarian for advice. Some of these kittens need further treatment for anemia.

Liver Cysts of Kittens

Occasionally cysts are found in livers of kittens. These are usually noticed as an incidental finding on an abdominal ultrasound. These cysts are like bubbles inside the liver. They are fluid filled and usually the size of a pea or marble. Since they don't really affect the liver tissue around them, you don't see symptoms and they don't need treated.

Portosystemic Shunts (PSS)

PSS is a complicated congenital defect. If you go back to the beginning of this chapter, I highlighted the different arteries and veins that profuse the liver. In a normal healthy kitten, these blood vessels keep the blood flowing from the intestines through the liver. This way the liver can filter out digestive by-products. In kittens born with PSS, the blood vessels are abnormal and disrupt the normal flow of blood through the liver. The aberrant blood vessels redirect the blood so it doesn't flow from the intestines through the liver, but circumvents the liver. This means that the blood from the intestines doesn't get filtered.

The symptoms caused by this disruption of the blood flow are:
- A small liver (small because it's no longer doing its full job)
- Underweight and small kittens
- Vomiting and diarrhea
- Neurological symptoms and bizarre behavior after eating
- Jaundice
- Elevated blood ammonia levels
- Elevated liver enzyme test results
- Delayed blood clotting
- Abnormal liver biopsies

The best way to diagnose these cases is through an ultrasound of the liver and the blood vessels that flow through it. Another way is to inject dye into the jugular vein and take x-rays as the dye circulates through the portal vessels (called *portovenography*). Treatment of the severe cases consists of tying off the abnormal blood vessel to restore normal circulation through the liver, which is a very difficult surgery that only a specialist veterinary surgeon should attempt.

Dietary management also is helpful for decreasing symptoms. Foods should be low in proteins, that is, a protein-restricted diet. Protein, if not synthesized by the liver can increase blood ammonia levels which leads to neurological symptoms. These kittens should be fed a carbohydrate-heavy diet with high fiber. A drug that helps lower blood ammonia levels is *lactulose*.

Disease Info Box

Disease	Liver disease
Common Symptoms	Jaundice, vomiting, neurological changes, weight loss
Diagnosis	X-ray, abdominal ultrasound, liver biopsy, blood tests
Treatment Options	Low protein diets, Lactulose, antibiotics, anti-inflammatory drugs, supportive care, surgery

Chapter 15

Neurological Problems

Kittens can get a whole host of brain and nervous system problems, collectively called *neurological disorders*. Some kittens are born with them while others acquire them via disease or poisoning. The majority of the neurological problems involve brain disorders. Please be aware that brain problems are serious and require prompt veterinary care. (The neurological problems of older cats are not addressed in this book.)

Infectious Neurological Diseases

Certain diseases that kittens get can cause neurological symptoms. The infectious organism—bacteria or virus—infects the brain or other nervous tissue. Most of these diseases are very serious; one in particular, rabies, is always fatal. Some cause permanent changes, others are temporary and treatable.

Cerebellar Hypoplasia

Kittens born of mothers infected with feline panleukopenia virus during pregnancy have an underdeveloped *cerebellum*. The cerebellum is the part of the brain that controls coordination of muscles, so these kittens have wildly swinging, jerking, trembling, uncoordinated body movements. The degree of incoordination can be so severe that the kitten cannot walk or use a litter box. In milder cases, kittens can function well enough to carry on normal daily functions. I have seen both. I have also had to euthanize severely afflicted kittens who couldn't walk or stand long enough to eat.

Symptoms usually appear shortly after the kittens start trying to walk, around four weeks of age. The good news is that the kittens don't generally get worse once symptoms start. This is an easy diagnosis for any veterinarian who has ever seen these kittens. Nothing else looks like it. No treatment is possible other than lot of TLC. Try to make things as easy as possible for your afflicted kitten. Use a low litter pan and food dishes. Don't make him go up or down stairs and always keep these him inside.

Cerebral Granuloma

Kittens infected with feline infectious peritonitis (FIP) can develop *granulomas* (lumps brought on by the virus) in the brain. The specific symptoms depend on the location of the lesion in the brain. The most common symptoms are seizures, paralysis, and blindness. Other symptoms of FIP usually are visible as well (see Chapter 2 for details). The diagnosis involves a blood test for the FIP virus as well as other diagnostic tests. Kittens with brain lesions have a poor chance of overcoming this disease. Consult with your veterinarian as to the best course of action. Please keep in mind that many kittens do not survive this.

Rabies

See Chapter 2.

Disease Info Box	
Disease	Infectious neurological diseases
Common Symptoms	Circling, blindness, seizure, tremors, incoordination
Diagnosis	Physical exam, blood tests, FIP test, brain biopsy, CAT scan
Treatment Options	Supportive for viral diseases, lots of TLC

Hydrocephalus

Hydrocephalus is a condition in which excess fluids build up and put pressure on the brain. The brain should always have a certain flow of normal fluid, called *cerebral spinal fluid* (CSF), which circulates between the brain and skull. The disease is fairly rare in kittens, but if you see a case of it, you never forget it. The skull and cranium are swollen and enlarged, with a distinct swelling on the top of the head. The CSF accumulation results from a failure of the fluid to drain out as new fluid flows into the space between the brain and skull.

The feline infectious peritonitis (FIP) virus has been shown to cause these increased intracranial pressure changes. These kittens show symptoms related to the pressure on the brain, such as blindness, circling and seizures. These symptoms occur within several weeks of age. The diagnosis is made on clinical signs and a skull x-ray. Nowadays, CAT (Computer Assisted

Topography) scans can clearly show the distended cranium with fluid accumulation displacing brain tissue. Treatment can range from careful observation to draining the fluid off the brain.

Disease Info Box

Disease	Hydrocephalus
Common Symptoms	Neurological signs, blindness, seizures
Diagnosis	X-ray, clinical symptoms, CAT scan
Treatment Options	Observation, aspirating fluid out of cranium

---

Seizures and Epilepsy

These are frightening disorders in which kittens have a spasm of uncontrollable involuntary muscle action. There are three different levels of seizures:

- **Petit Mal.**   Short-lived and mild seizures that often involve only one part of the body, such as the jaw, eyelid, one leg, or tail.

- **Grand Mal.**   Longer and more severe seizures that often involve the whole body and cause the animal to fall over, shake, kick, vocalize, and void urine or stool. The animal usually loses consciousness.

- **Status Epilepticus.**   A chain of grand mal seizures with little respite between them. Can be dangerous and immediately life-threatening.

Several different factors cause seizures in kittens. Some of the more common causes are listed below:

- Epilepsy—seizures of unknown cause
- Head trauma with increased intracranial pressure
- Liver disease (see hepatic encephalopathy, later in this chapter)
- Heat stroke
- Hypoglycemia (low blood sugar)
- Poisonings (furniture polish, Yew shrub berries, charcoal lighter fluid, chocolate, kerosene, lead, paint thinner, and strychnine)
- Toxoplasmosis
- Viral diseases—feline infectious peritonitis (FIP), feline leukemia virus (FeLV), feline immunodeficiency virus (FIV)

All seizures show a few consistent features, whatever the cause. Most animals feel the seizure coming on and might cling to you out of fear. Most seizures are short, meaning the actual convulsive phase lasts only a few minutes.

After the seizure ends, the animal feels dazed and disoriented for as long as several hours. Weakness and dullness often characterize the post-seizure period.

Diagnosis of feline seizures usually involves doing a complete blood workup including blood tests for FeLV, FIV, and FIP. A complete physical exam is done in the hopes of finding a physical abnormality such as a heart murmur. Treatment really depends on the underlying cause of the seizures. Several anti-seizure drugs can help lessen the severity of the seizure by shortening it or making it milder. Cases of poisoning must be treated with things to absorb the toxins, like activated charcoal.

Disease Info Box

Disease	Seizures and epilepsy
Common Symptoms	Convulsions
Diagnosis	Screening blood workup, physical exam, FeLV, FIP, FIV and Toxoplasma test, toxicology blood tests
Treatment Options	Anti-seizure drugs, treat underlying organic disease

Lead Poisoning

Cats are very susceptible to lead poisoning, just like children. Lead can come in the form of lead paint, plumbing solder, grease, fishing weights, buckshot, or lead contaminated water. Lead is very toxic to blood cells and nerve tissues. Lead-poisoned kittens have profound anemia (low red blood cell count), red blood cell changes seen on a blood smear, vomiting, diarrhea, and neurological symptoms like seizures, coma, and blindness. The diagnosis is made by running a complete blood count and blood lead level. Treatment usually consists of supportive intravenous fluids and a *chelating* (binding) compound that binds with the lead to bring down the blood and brain levels. These cases must be watched closely for further complications.

Disease Info Box

Disease	Lead poisoning
Common Symptoms	Neurological signs, blindness, seizures, coma, vomiting and diarrhea
Diagnosis	Complete blood count, blood lead level
Treatment Options	IV fluids, lead chelating agents

Hepatic Encephalopathy

Kittens who have a failing liver can have neurological symptoms. Chapter 14, "Liver Diseases," discusses causes of liver disease in kittens. Regardless of the actual cause of the liver failure, the levels of blood ammonia increase to the point of being toxic to brain tissue. One of the most common liver disorders that leads to hepatic encephalopathy is portosystemic shunts (discussed in Chapter 14). The symptoms are of both liver failure—jaundice, vomiting, weight loss, elevated blood liver enzyme tests, elevated bile acid tests—and neurological disturbances—blindness, circling, seizures, coma. The symptoms usually are worse after a high protein meal, because protein breaks down to ammonia, which is released in the blood.

Disease Info Box	
Disease	Hepatic encephalopathy
Common Symptoms	Neurological signs, blindness, seizures, coma, jaundice
Diagnosis	Liver ultrasound, blood ammonia levels
Treatment Options	Low protein diets, lactulose

Chapter 16

Blood
Disorders

lood is an essential fluid that circulates throughout the tissues of the body, delivering oxygen, hormones, nutrients, and electrolytes while removing toxins and waste products. Blood is composed of three components: blood cells (red, white, and platelets), serum (the most liquid fraction without clotting components), and plasma (a combination of serum plus clotting components). The red blood cells come from the bone marrow and spleen and carry oxygen to body tissues. White blood cells come from the bone marrow and lymph nodes and make up the immune system. Platelets are the cells that form blood clots.

If any components of blood are out of balance, serious problems can results. If red blood cells are deficient, for instance, the tissues don't properly oxygenate. If white blood cells are deficient, the kitten has an impaired immune system and is susceptible to infections. If platelets are low, the kitten has prolonged clotting times. This chapter covers disorders of blood. Some are genetic, some are from poisonings, and some are caused by disease.

Anemia

Anemia is the lack of red blood cells. A kitten can lose red blood cells in three basic ways:

- Blood loss through a cut or wound, internal worms that drain blood, external parasites like fleas, or parasites of red blood cells themselves, like *hemobartonella felis*.

- Insufficient red blood cells manufactured by the bone marrow or spleen, usually owing to viral diseases like feline leukemia virus (FeLV) and feline immunodeficiency virus (FIV).

- Destruction by by disease or drugs, or by the kitten's own immune system, as in *autoimmune hemolytic anemia* (AIHA).

Diagnosis of anemia involves a CBC (Complete Blood Count) test, which gives counts and percentages of red, white, and platelet cells. If the percentage of red blood cells falls below 15 percent, the kitten's life can be at risk and a blood transfusion might be necessary. In more mild cases, vitamin and iron supplements might be enough to raise the red blood cell count to normal levels, between 32–35 percent. A fecal exam should be run for the presence of internal parasites, as well as a thorough physical exam to look for bleeding wounds or fleas. A blood test for FeLV and FIV should be run promptly, too, because of these diseases' ability to suppress the bone marrow.

Treatment involves correcting the underlying disease or poisoning. Obviously, a bleeding wound must be stopped immediately! Also, just as obviously, if your kitten has worms or fleas, they must be treated. Unfortunately, no easy cure exists for the viral diseases that cause anemia and bone marrow suppression.

Disease Info Box

Disease	Anemia
Common Symptoms	Low red blood cell counts
Diagnosis	Physical exam, complete blood count, fecal exam, FeLV and FIV test
Treatment Options	Worming, flea baths, vitamin and iron supplements, blood transfusions

Chediak-Higashi Syndrome of Persians

This is an inherited disease of Persian cats with a gray or blue coat color. These kittens have a form of hemophilia with delayed blood clotting. They also have impaired immune systems because the white blood cells are defective. The only way to diagnose these kittens is to have a microscopic examination of a blood smear. The pathologist can see the defective white blood cells and platelets. This defect is genetic and untreatable. These kittens should be watched carefully for infections and unusual bleeding tendencies.

Disease Info Box

Disease	Chediak-Higashi Syndrome
Common Symptoms	Delayed clotting, impaired immune response
Diagnosis	Blood smea cytology exam
Treatment Options	None

Hemobartonellosis

Hemobartonella felis is an infectious bacteria of feline red blood cells. Insect bites can spread the disease. The parasite infects red blood cells and alters them enough so that the kitten's immune system destroys the blood cells, which leads to anemia. The pathologist diagnoses these cases with a microscopic exam of a blood smear. They can actually see the bacteria on the red blood cells. There are those who think that *hemobartonella* is a major cause of *autoimmune hemolytic anemia*, a disease in which the kitten's own immune system destroys its red blood cells. Hemobartonellosis often occurs in conjunction with feline leukemia virus or feline immunodeficiency virus.

The affected kittens are pale, anemic, and have high fevers over 104°F. The blood cell destruction also can lead to jaundice, a yellowing of the mucus membranes. Treatment is with antibiotics of the tetracycline family and cortisone to reduce the immune destruction of the red blood cells.

Disease Info Box

Disease	Hemobartonellosis
Common Symptoms	Anemia, pale mucus membranes, fever
Diagnosis	Physical exam, CBC, blood smears
Treatment Options	Tetracycline antibiotics, vitamins, iron supplements, cortisone

Patterns in Blood Counts

As you will find out, any time your kittens gets sick or runs a fever, your veterinarian might want to run a complete blood count (CBC) to determine whether appropriate numbers of the different types of blood cells are circulating in the blood. This information can be very valuable, for the following reasons:

- An increase in red blood cells often means dehydration
- A decrease in red blood cells is anemia (see section above)
- An increase in white blood cells often means a bacterial infection or a blood cancer
- A decrease in white blood cells often means viral infection or bone marrow suppression

During times of stress, such as being in an animal hospital and getting blood drawn, cats can have an artificial change in their blood counts, called a *stress pattern*. Your veterinarian should take these into consideration when interpreting the CBC.

Tylenol Toxicity

There are many common household drugs that are toxic to cats. The most common are *acetaminophen*, or Tylenol, and *aspirin*.

Acetaminophen causes toxic changes to a cat's blood, altering the red blood cell's ability to carry oxygen to the tissues. The drug leads to anemia, poor oxygenation, and red blood cell destruction. Liver damage often is noted as well. These cats breathe heavy, are very pale, have fast heart rates, and ruddy looking mucus membranes. Treatment often begins by inducing the kitten to vomit the ingested drug. After that, drugs are available to counteract the acetaminophen, but your veterinarian has to give them promptly, usually within hours of the ingestion of the acetaminophen.

Aspirin is another common household medication that is toxic to kittens. Aspirin upsets a kitten's stomach and can lead to vomiting. It also decreases blood cells and blood clotting. The clinical symptoms are very similar to acetaminophen poisoning, showing gastritis, breathing distress, and anemia. The treatment is to induce vomiting to treat the upset stomach and then provide supportive care.

Disease Info Box

Disease	Acetaminophen and aspirin toxicity
Common Symptoms	Breathing distress, anemia, liver failure, vomiting
Diagnosis	CBC, liver enzyme tests, blood smear
Treatment Options	Induce vomiting, supportive care, oxygen therapy

Viral Bone Marrow Suppression

The bone marrow sometimes doesn't produce normal numbers of red and white blood cells. To review, red blood cells are the cells in the blood that carry oxygen to bodily tissues. The white blood cells make up a large part of the kitten's immune system. Any disease or disorder that affects the bone marrow's ability to produce these cells will lead to the following problems:

- If red blood cell production decreases, anemia results.
- If white blood cell production decreases, the kitten's immune response is suppressed.

Three viral diseases are known to cause bone marrow suppression, anemia, and reduced white blood cells: feline leukemia virus, feline immunodeficiency virus, and feline panleukopenia virus (Chapter 2 offers a complete description of each of these viruses). Affected kittens are very prone to bacterial, parasitic, and fungal infections owing to the impairment of their immune systems. Systemic antibiotics and/or anti-fungal drugs can reduce bacterial and fungal infections. Parasitic infections need appropriate anthelmintic medications.

I have many patients who have one or more of these viral infections. Their health is certainly a roller coaster—ups and downs, good days and bad. The owners are saints for all the time, effort, and TLC they provide to keep these cats alive and well. Early diagnosis and treatment of any ailment, no matter how small, is key. You have to decide how devoted you are if your kitten should come down with one of these immunosuppressive viruses. I'm sure with the help of your veterinarian you will do the best you can. Remember, it's the effort that's rewarding.

Disease Info Box

Disease	Bone marrow suppression
Common Symptoms	Reduced white blood cells, frequent infections, anemia
Diagnosis	Physical exam, CBC, FeLV, FIV, Panleukopenia tests
Treatment Options	Supportive care, systemic antibiotic, anti-fungal, anthelmintic drugs

Chapter 17

Hormonal Problems

There aren't many disruptions in a kitten's hormone system, also called the *endocrine system*. Hormones are substances that have certain functions to perform as they circulate in the bloodstream. The following are some examples:

- The *thyroid* gland secretes thyroid hormone, which maintains the body's metabolism

- The *pituitary* gland secretes several hormones, which maintain cell integrity, water balance, natural cortisone level, sex characteristics, and body size, respectively

- The *gonads* (sex parts) secrete sex hormones

- The *pancreas* secretes insulin for blood sugar regulation

When one of these hormone glands malfunctions, a related bodily function falls out of whack. Two hormonal disruptions are commonly seen in kittens: hypoglycemia and diabetes.

Hypoglycemia

Hypoglycemia literally means low blood sugar. Several factors can bring about low blood sugar. One of the most prevalent is malnutrition. If a kitten isn't eating properly or regularly enough, the blood sugar can drop to dangerously low levels. Another reason a kitten might develop low blood sugar would be a severe case of parasites that continuously rob him of nutrition. A third reason involves a hormonal imbalance that causes a drop of blood sugar. The *pancreas gland* secretes *insulin*, a hormone that regulates blood glucose levels. An increase in the insulin levels causes blood glucose to drop.

176

The blood sugar, *glucose*, comes from carbohydrates in food. The carbo-hydrates are converted to glucose, which is the sugar that the body cells needs for energy. Without a proper level of blood sugar, the body organs cannot perform their functions, leading to multiple organ system failure with varied symptoms. The most common symptoms are dizziness, incoordination, disorientation, confusion, and seizures.

Your veterinarian will run a blood glucose level to diagnose these cases. Depending on the results, your kitten might need intravenous sugar, usually *dextrose*, to raise the blood to normal levels. Frequent small meals also help to stabilize blood glucose levels.

Disease Info Box

Disease	Hypoglycemia
Common Symptoms	Dizziness, incoordination, disorientation, seizures
Diagnosis	Blood glucose levels, blood insulin levels
Treatment Options	Frequent small meals, pancreatic tumor removal

Diabetes Mellitus (Sugar Diabetes)

This is a hormonal disease that involves the kitten's inability to regulate his own blood sugar. Kittens who have *juvenile diabetes* have a deficiency of *insulin* secreted by the pancreas gland. The cats most prone to diabetes are overweight male cats. Insulin is the hormone that lowers blood glucose after a meal. An insufficient amount of insulin or an inability to utilize insulin results in blood glucose increasing to high levels after eating, usually exceeding 250 milligrams per deciliter (mg/dl). After the sugar reaches that level, it spills out of the blood and into the urine. Then both blood and urine glucose levels are elevated.

Normally, on an empty stomach, the blood glucose level of a kitten is relatively low. After a meal, the blood sugar rises. The pancreas releases insulin to pull the glucose out of the blood and into the body cells, lowering the blood sugar back to pre-meal levels. This process can take several hours.

What happens in a diabetic animal is quite different. After a meal, the blood glucose level rises, no insulin pulls it down, so it keeps rising. *The body cells cannot utilize the glucose because, without the insulin, it stays in the blood.*

If all the sugar is in the blood, the body cells don't get the fuel they need, causing a total body system breakdown. Basically, these kittens are starving to death even with all that sugar floating around in their blood! Symptoms other than starvation include dehydration owing to excessive urinations; increased thirst; weight loss; kidney failure; an acidy smell to breath; cataracts; muscle weakness; and eventual coma and death.

The standard treatment for diabetes in animals is injections of whatever insulin hormone their system lacks. There are different types of insulin, but one of the most commonly used types of insulin in cats is NPH insulin. NPH insulin and has two peaks of action, about 8 hours apart. NPH often is given just once a day, first thing in the morning, but can be given twice daily.

Glucose takes a nose dive starting within an hour of the insulin injection. It also causes a sharp drop eight hours later, as is characteristic for NPH insulin. If the dose is correct, the glucose never drops below the minimum level. There are ways to keep the blood glucose from dropping too much, the easiest and most practical is to feed your kitten at strategic times. Longer-acting insulins are now available.

An owner of a diabetic cat must do a rather complicated procedure every day to give the cat its proper dose of insulin, which is outlined in the accompanying sidebar. Your veterinarian will be able to guide you through until you're comfortable treating the kitten yourself.

Guidelines for Treating a Diabetic Kitten

- Check the urine glucose every morning with a dipstick
- Compare urine stick reading to your chart to determine the proper amount of insulin for that day
- Give insulin shot subcutaneously in morning
- Feed your kitten immediately following the insulin injection, then eight hours later
- Keep a journal of the urine glucose readings and insulin units given each day
- Watch your kitten for an hour after the insulin injection for signs of insulin shock
- Always keep Karo syrup handy in case he has insulin shock

Insulin Shock

Too much insulin causes a very sudden and sharp decline in the blood glucose level, which initially leads to stupor, weakness, and disorientation. Minutes later, it can lead to twitching and seizures, which must be treated immediately. The first thing to do is spread some pancake syrup or Karo sweetener on your kitten's gums. Do this every five minutes and call your veterinarian.

Disease Info Box

Disease	Diabetes mellitus
Common Symptoms	Increased thirst and urinations, weight loss, acidy smell to breath, weakness, dehydration
Diagnosis	Blood glucose levels, urine glucose levels
Treatment Options	Insuling injections, high fiber diets, hypoglycemic drugs, weight loss

Chapter 18

Orthopedic Problems

This chapter reviews the orthopedic problems kittens can have. Some of these problems the kitten is born with, while others are trauma-induced injuries. I cover the birth defects first, then shift into the traumatic cases. Keep in mind that they all affect bones, joints, or muscles in some way.

Orthopedic Birth Defects

Bone and joint defects are noticeable shortly after birth. The kitten doesn't run or jump like it should. She might have a limp or a weakness. It's usually obvious to anyone who sees her that something's wrong. This section examines the possible causes for the problem.

Angular Deformity

Angular deformity is a condition in which the long bones of the arms and legs fail to develop straight, and have a curvature to them. Long bones of the fore and hind limbs grow by elongating at both ends. This happens at the *growth plate* zones. These are areas at both ends of the bone that produce new bone. If one of these growth plates of a bone stops producing new bone (called *premature closure*) while the other end is still elongating, the bone bends. If two bones are connected at both ends (as in the radius-ulna of the forelimb, or the tibia-fibula of the hind limb), and one growth plate closes, the limb bends or bows.

Closure of each different growth plate causes different variations of angular deformities. If the growth plate above the wrist of the ulna bone prematurely closes, for example, but the radius continues to grow, the forelimb bows forward and the wrist turns outward.

If the angulation is mild, no treatment is needed. For cases that produce a limp, casts or splints might be enough to correct the deviation. These should be done before the bones completely calcify, so before the kitten reaches six months of age. If the angulation is severe enough to cause a deformity of the limb, surgical treatment should be attempted by six months. The orthopedic surgeon removes a wedge of bone (*osteotomy* is the name of the procedure) from the curved side of the bone and then rigidly fixes the bone ends with internal hardware, like a bone plate and screws. This procedure requires great expertise, and only a qualified surgeon should attempt it. Done right, a functional limb results, although the limb might be slightly shorter than its other side.

Polydactyly Toes

Polydactyly toes isn't so much a birth defect as a natural variation. Affected kittens have more than the normal five toes, usually in the front paws, although they can occur in the hind also. These kittens can have up to seven toes on each paw! This is a genetic trait. The large paws look like baseball mitts, but are of little consequence to the kitten. Other names for this condition are "double paws," and "extra toes." Occasionally one of the extra toenails can become ingrown, meaning the nail grows into the pad, so don't forget to trim *all* the nails during a nail cutting.

Swimmer Kittens

These kittens are born with a birth defect of the ribcage and sternum (breast bone) and its associated musculature, causing the kitten to collapse when trying to stand. Their chest appears caved in. They paddle their legs trying to

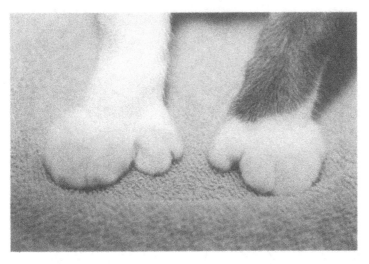

A kitten with polydactyl toes, often called "mitts."

get up, but they look like they're swimming, hence the name. These kittens appear neurologically normal but can have breathing distress. They need physical therapy to strengthen their pectoral muscles and, in severe cases, corrective surgery. This does seem to be an inherited defect.

Dwarfism (Munchkin)

This really is a hormonal problem, but I included it in this chapter rather than Chapter 18 because it *looks* like an orthopedic disorder. Actually, it's both. Kittens born with a deficiency of *growth hormone*, which is one of the hormones responsible for growth of long bones, end up dwarfed. These kittens have normal looking bodies, but very, very short legs. In fact, the ones that I see at my office might only be six inches tall! Munchkins make wonderful pets, and seem healthy otherwise, although they cannot jump, climb, or run like a normal kitten.

Kinked Tail

Some kittens are born with a kink, or hook at the tip of their tail. It's not a health obstacle, but it can prevent a kitten from becoming a show cat. Most breeders don't breed cats who have kinked tails for fear that they'll pass the trait on to their kittens.

Cranial Cruciate Sprain or Rupture

The cruciate ligament is the main ligament that holds the knee joint (the *stifle*) together. The stifle consits of three bones: the *femur* (upper leg bone), the *tibia* (the lower leg bone), and the *patella*, or knee cap. The cruciate

Notice the very short legs on this Munchkin kitten. This is a form of dwarfism.

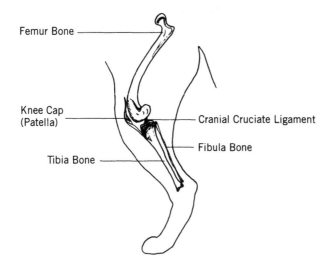

Femur Bone

Knee Cap
(Patella)

Tibia Bone

Cranial Cruciate Ligament

Fibula Bone

The cruciate ligament is what holds the knee joint together,
as seen in this diagram of a normal feline patella (knee).

ligament keeps the femur from sliding over the tibia bone. Kittens are prone
to injuring their knees from falling out of trees or other accidents.

Twisting motion is the most common cause of tearing this. With the feet
planted firmly on the ground and the upper body twisting (say to catch a
bird), the cruciate ligament is stressed. If the ligament is stretched, or
partially torn, it results in a *sprain*, and immediate pain in the joint. The
lameness can be anywhere from a slight limp to a major case in which any
weight on the leg at all is unbearable.

Diagnosis is made by observing the cat walk, checking for a *draw sign* and
an x-ray. The draw sign is a technique veterinarians use to detect laxity in the
knee joint. The vet tries to slide the upper femur bone over the lower tibia
while the knee is slightly flexed. If the two bones slide over one another, it's
considered a positive draw sign, and the diagnosis is cruciate rupture. Complete
ruptures of the ligament have a more dramatic draw sign. An x-ray is taken if a
complete rupture is suspected. If the rupture is complete, the end of the torn
ligament takes a small piece of bone with it (called an *Avulsed bone fragment*).
This is noticeable on the x-ray and diagnostic for a complete rupture.

Treatment varies depending on whether the rupture was partial or
complete. Also, different vets treat these differently. The following table
summarizes treatment options for both conditions.

Type of Cruciate Damage	Treatment Options
Cruciate ligament sprain	Limit exercise Anti-inflammatory drugs
Complete cruciate rupture	Splints Padded bandages Cage rest Surgery Physical therapy Rehabilitation

Disease Info Box

Disease	Cruciate ligament sprain
Treatment	Limit exercise, anti-inflammatory drugs
Disease	Complete cruciate rupture
Treatment Options	Surgery, physical therapy, rehabilitation

Partial tears and ruptures generally heal without surgery. This might mean weeks in a bandage or splint, and complete rest, followed by a month or two of reduced activity. Ice packs serve to reduce acute swelling (within the first 12 hours), then moist, warm heat thereafter. Complete rest means staying inside and not going up or down stairs. Often you have to put your kitten in a crate or cage to limit his activity.

Most kittens heal very quickly and usually repair their ligaments much faster than do people. Any splint applied to a growing kitten's leg must be changed frequently to allow for the expanding limb, or becomes constrictive. You might have to make litter box accommodations for the splint, especially if you have a covered litter box.

The surgery to repair a complete cruciate rupture involves reconstruction of the ligament. The joint is opened and inspected for an avulsed bone fragment. Any found are removed. Several different surgical techniques are used. Some surgeons utilize the patellar ligament to reconstruct the cruciate ligament. Others use manmade materials like surgical stainless steel wire or nylon heavy gauge suture. If done well, the surgery is an excellent way to restore almost complete function. Post-operative considerations include a several week recovery period and the chance of arthritis in the knee joint months to years down the road.

Disease Info Box

Disease	Cranial cruciate rupture
Common Symptoms	Pronounced lameness, swelling and pain of knee
Diagnosis	Physical exam, draw sign, x-ray
Treatment Options	Rest, splinting, surgical repair

Muscle Strains, Pulls, and Cramps

Everyone sometime or another overdoes an activity or motion, causing a muscle strain or pull. Kittens are so active that they often pull something. First, take a look at the injury in more detail to get an idea of what's really happening.

Muscles are made of many, many stringy fibers that slide over each over to form a contraction. They are highly vascular with many arteries and veins. Nerves run through the muscles to control each and every contraction. Each muscle fiber is covered with a sheet of fibrous tissue, limiting the extent to which it can contract. When these limits are pushed, or ignored, damage to the muscle fibers results. If the damage is extensive, bleeding can occur within the muscle, leading to swelling and bruising. Inflammation quickly follows the tear to the muscle fibers. Swelling and pain ensues, which can last for days to weeks.

Cramping is not as dramatic. Muscle cramps occur when there is oxygen deprivation to the muscle or a buildup of *lactic acid*, which is a byproduct of muscle contraction. Cramps usually are temporary, lasting only minutes. The muscle is in an involuntary spasm which is very painful while it lasts, but quickly relieves itself.

Kittens are prone to sprains from climbing trees, jumping over fences, or hunting. Within an hour, a muscle, or group of muscles, swells and becomes painful. Hind leg and thigh muscles are common places for sprains. The shoulder and neck also are common areas.

Treatment isn't necessary in mild cases. In more severe ones, anti-inflammatory drugs, warm and moist compresses, and rest are the best remedies. If a muscle is actually torn, it can take weeks or months to recover completely.

Disease Info Box

Disease	Muscle sprains, pulls, and cramps
Common Symptoms	Muscle swelling, pain, lameness
Diagnosis	Physical exam
Treatment Options	Rest, anti-inflammatory drugs, warm compress

---

Tendon Strain

Tendonitis is defined as inflammation of the tendons. Tendons are the fibrous bands that connect the muscles to bone. All muscles are connected at both ends to bones by their tendons. If enough stress is placed on the tendon, the filaments of the tendon can tear. These injuries are very common from heavy play or activity. Any tendon is susceptible to straining. The first symptom of a strained tendon is acute pain and swelling at the site of injury. X-rays are normal since no orthopedic damage occurs to the bone structure.

Veterinarians grade lameness in animals on a scale of 1 to 5, with 1 being barely noticeable and 5 meaning the animal won't use the leg at all. These kittens usually present as 1 or 2 on the lameness scale.

Treatment consists of ice packs to reduce acute swelling (within the first 12 hours), then moist warm heat from then on. A soft padded bandage might be needed to help splint and support the damaged muscle and tendon. Resting the injury is essential for proper healing. This means staying inside, not jumping on and off of the window sill. The owner must abide by these rules, or the tendon won't heal or will take a very long time to return to normal.

Disease Info Box

Disease	Tendon strain
Common Symptoms	Acute swelling of tendon, pain, lameness
Diagnosis	Physical exam, x-ray
Treatment Options	Rest, anti-inflammatory drugs, ice packs immediately, warm compress later, padded bandages

---

Fractures

A fracture simply means a broken bone. There are many different ways a bone can break. The way a bone breaks depends on the forces or strain that causes the break. Not all breaks are the same, but when a fracture occurs, regardless of which kind, the symptoms are similar:

- Pain and swelling at the site of fracture
- Immediate lameness, with the kitten not using the leg
- Limb possibly dangling or dragging behind the others
- Crunching noise heard when manipulating the leg

Your veterinarian makes the diagnosis by feeling the leg at the site at which the fracture is suspected. Ultimately, an x-ray is needed to differentiate between the type of fractures. After reading the x-rays, he or she makes recommendations concerning treatment, which could range from a padded bandage, to a cast, to surgery.

Before bones can heal, the two ends must be brought together to touch each other, called *reduction* of the fracture. Sometimes this can be done just by manipulating the leg (called closed reduction). Other times it must be done surgically under anesthesia if the muscles are contracting keeping the two ends of the bone separated (called open reduction).

To heal, the bone ends must be kept together and absolutely still, called *immobilization* of the fracture site. Bone ends cannot heal if there is motion. Therefore, the fracture site must be made stable by one of two means: external fixation or internal fixation.

External Fixation: Casts and Splints

Casts and splints are stiff bandages that keep fractures immobile. They are best used on lower extremities of the legs. Years ago, casts were made of Plaster of Paris. Today, most of them are either fiberglass, or sectioned from prefab plastic. The advantage to fiberglass or plastic casting is that they're lightweight, waterproof, and easy to apply and remove. Splints are usually made of pliable aluminum strips or rods. Casts and splints can stay on anywhere from 4–12 weeks, depending on which bone is fractured, and how badly. Keeping them dry and soil free is the hardest part. Most cats tolerate them but can limp for a few

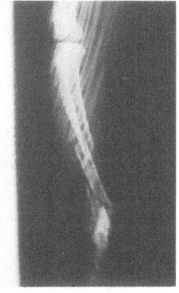

X-ray of a fractured hind leg. This is a closed fracture.

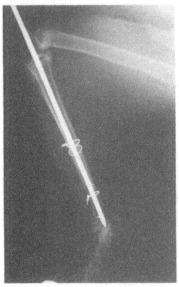

X-ray of a fracture repaired with an intramedulary pin and wires.

weeks until they get used to the idea. Cats often try to "flick" off the splint with a quick shaking of the leg. In a young kitten, any type of bandage would need to be changed frequently in order to allow room for growth or it will get too tight and cut off the circulation to the leg.

Internal Fixation: Hardware

When a fracture is not a good candidate for external fixation, the other alternative is internal fixation. Internal fixation is a surgical alternative. Again, the same principles apply: you must have complete immobilization at the fracture site for it to heal.

The actual hardware consists of wires, screws, intramedullary pins (rods that insert down the middle of the bone shaft), bone plates, and external Kirschner rods that support from the outside.

Common Kitten Fractures

There are a few common orthopedic problems that kittens get other than the leg fractures described above. These are usually seen in outdoor cats, except for the last one, high rise syndrome, in which a cat thinks he's a bird.

Jaw Fracture

A jaw fracture usually comes from falling out of a tree or being kicked. The jaw usually fractures right in the center where the left and right halves join (called the mandibular symphysis). These are corrected by wrapping a stainless steel wire around the base of the teeth to stabilize the fracture site.

Pelvic Fracture

Pelvic fractures usually come from being hit by a car. A pelvis can fracture in many different places. Some are very serious and require surgery. Others aren't serious and just require cage rest for several weeks.

Tail Fracture

Tail fractures usually come about from getting caught in a door. The fracture isn't really a fracture, because a single bone is not broken. It is really more of a dislocation of the vertebrae of the tail. The tail is bent at the dislocation and can be very painful. If the dislocation is close to the base of the tail, it can cause nerve damage, leaving a paralyzed tail. A dead tail is bad because the kitten can't control his tail and is always getting it caught in doors and getting messy in the litter box. Treatment consists of splinting the fracture site, or in cases of paralysis, amputating the tail.

High Rise Syndrome

High rise syndrome usually results from jumping out of an upper story window. Cats have an uncanny ability to fall from high places and survive because of their balance and ability to right themselves in midair. They do not escape injury, however. The following list enumerates some common injuries seen in high rise syndrome:

- Nose bleeds (from head hitting ground)
- Split roof of mouth (from head hitting ground)
- Fractured ulna bones above the wrist of both front legs
- Fractured ribs with breathing distress
- Broken teeth

The best treatment for this condition is immediate veterinary care.

Disease Info Box

Disease	Fractures
Common Symptoms	Acute swelling and pain, lameness
Diagnosis	Physical exam, x-ray
Treatment Options	Cage rest, internal or external fixation, splints or casts

Dislocations

A dislocation (also called a luxation) is when a bone pops out of its joint. The joint is usually damaged in the process: ligaments and connective tissue that hold the joint together are torn, promoting acute inflammation, pain, and swelling. Most owners can see that something's wrong with the cat because the swelling or angulation appears where it doesn't belong. These are painful to the touch, and I would leave the poking and prodding to the veterinarian.

The joints that are most prone to dislocation are the shoulder, hip, knee, hock and temporal mandibular (jaw). The most common in cats is the hip, as detailed in the following section. The diagnosis is made by palpating the injured joint and an x-ray. Depending on which joint, your kitten could need strict cage rest, a splint or cast, or even surgery to reduce the dislocation (pop the bone back in the joint). Either way, you can expect mild arthritis to set in months to years later.

Dislocated Hip

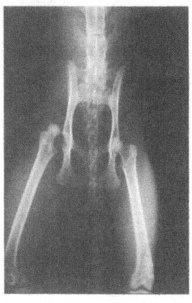

This dislocation is usually a result of being hit by a car. These cats cannot walk on the affected leg without a severe limp. It is very painful to manipulate the hip. What happens is that the head of the femur (called the "ball") pops out of the socket in the pelvis. The best treatment is to anesthetize the cat and place the hip back into the socket. If all

X-ray of a dislocated hip. You can see the ball of the femur on the left hip is out of the socket.

the ligaments and connective tissue that holds the head in the socket are torn, it will pop right out again. In this case, the two alternatives are to surgically repair the dislocation or leave the head out of the socket. In cats, this heals on its own by forming a new "false" hip joint, called *pseudoarthrosis*. This leaves the cat with a permanently short leg and a limp.

Disease Info Box	
Disease	Dislocations
Common Symptoms	Acute swelling and pain, lameness
Diagnosis	Physical exam, x-ray
Treatment Options	Cage rest, splints or casts, surgical reduction

Chapter 19

Urinary Diseases

This chapter covers the most common diseases of a kitten's urinary system. The urinary system is made up of the kidneys, ureters (the tubes that carry the urine from the kidneys to the urinary bladder), urinary bladder, and urethra (the tube that carries urine out of the body).

The chapter progresses through the system from the kidneys and ends with the urethra. This is a very important chapter because urinary disease is common in kittens. Much of the urinary tract disease I see is a result of self-contamination from the litter box.

Urinary Tract Infection

Kidney and urinary bladder infections are very common in young animals. This is because they often soil themselves with urine and feces. This in turn leads to a contamination of the vulva (in a female) or the penis (in a male). The bacteria can make their way up the urethra and migrate into the urinary bladder with ease. Once there, the bacteria can colonize the wall of the bladder causing inflammation, bleeding, irritation and pain. Infections of the

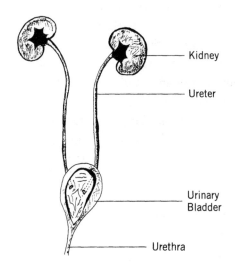

Kidney

Ureter

Urinary Bladder

Urethra

Diagram of the urinary system.

191

urinary bladder are called *cystitis*. Kittens with cystitis have very noticeable symptoms:

- Frequent urinations
- Straining to urinate (called *stranguria*)
- Crying out when urinating
- Blood-tinged urine (called *hematuria*)

Often these kittens become temporarily *incontinent*, or unable to hold their urine. This leads to urine staining of their fur and a urine smell about them. By now most people realize something is wrong with their kitten.

Your veterinarian will want a urine sample when you go in for a visit. A urine sample is sent to the laboratory for a *urinalysis*, which is a series of tests performed on the urine to determine the presence of blood, pus, pH, crystals, ketones, urobilinogen, bacteria and others. A urinalysis is critical to properly diagnose a urinary tract infection, so it is well worth the trouble you may have getting it.

There are two ways to get a urine sample from a kitten. 1) Get a plastic bead litter from your vet and substitute his regular litter with that. The beads don't absorb the urine, allowing you to collect it and pour it in a clean container. 2) Shred wax paper and substitute that for his regular litter—wax paper doesn't absorb urine, either.

Diagnostic tests other than a urinalysis can be performed to diagnose a urinary bladder infection is to take an x-ray of the bladder, looking for other problems, like bladder stones (cover below). There are special x-rays available where *radiopaque dye* (a special dye that you can readily see on an x-ray) is injected into the bladder to outline the inside, but these often require general anesthesia in a kitten. More useful than any x-ray is an ultrasound of the bladder, which is an extremely good for visualizing urinary bladder problems. Ultimately, a bladder biopsy can also diagnose tricky cases, but general anesthesia is needed and most often a biopsy is overkill for most bladder diseases.

If a urinary bladder is ignored, or goes unnoticed, it can turn into an infection of the kidneys (called *Pyelonephritis*). This is due to the continued migration of the bacterial up the urinary tract until they reach the kidneys. Once the infection is into to the kidneys, the severity of the disease becomes worse. Kittens with kidney infections have all of the same symptoms of a bladder infection, plus these:

- Fever
- Loss of appetite
- Lower abdominal pain

- Vomiting

- Pus in urine

These kittens are much sicker and are at risk of developing kidney failure (see below). The diagnosis of a kidney infection is the same as for cystitis, except the x-rays and ultrasound need to include the kidneys as well as the urinary bladder. Blood tests are also run to determine if the kidneys are still functioning properly (see below under *Kidney Failure*).

Treatment of either cystitis or kidney infections are treated with long term antibiotics to reduce the bacterial population. Urine acidifiers, such as vitamin C (ascorbic acid), lower the pH of urine and lower bacterial and yeast counts. Fluids should be encouraged to help flush out the bladder. This may mean giving your kitten chicken broth, skim milk, or even lightly salting his food with table salt to encourage water drinking. Most kittens respond quickly to these treatments. As always, kittens that do not respond to normal treatments should be checked for diseases that suppress their immune systems, like Feline Leukemia virus and Feline Immunodeficiency virus.

Disease Info Box	
Disease	Urinary tract infections
Common Symptoms	Stranguria, hematuria, painful urinations, incontinence
Diagnosis	Urinalysis, x-ray, ultrasound, blood tests
Treatment Options	Antibiotics, urine acidifiers, increase fluids

Kidney Failure

This section covers *acute kidney failure* only. Acute kidney failure is a *sudden* shut down of the kidneys due to either disease or poisoning. Chronic kidney failure is a slow failure of the kidneys which typically occurs in older cats.

There are three common causes for acute kidney failure in kittens, 1) kidney infection as described above, 2) antifreeze poisoning, and 3) urinary tract obstruction. Kidney infections were covered in the above section. Urinary tract obstruction is covered below under *Feline Urological Syndrome (FUS)*. I will detail antifreeze toxicity later in this section.

In most cases of sudden kidney failure, the kitten starts showing symptoms that are quite dramatic:

- Sudden increase in thirst, almost to the point of being obsessed with water

- No drinking with very little urine output several days into the disease
- Hematuria (blood in urine)
- Pyuria (pus in urine)
- Anemia
- Weight loss
- Lack of energy
- Oral blisters in the mouth

Diagnosis is made with blood tests for kidney function. The Blood Urea Nitrogen (BUN) and Creatinine tests are specific for kidneys. Abdominal x-rays and ultrasound can also help diagnose kidney failure. A urinalysis can also show evidence of kidney failure. The concentration of the urine (called the *Specific Gravity*) is very low; almost water-like. This is because the kidney has lost its ability to concentrate the urine and conserve water for the body. In cats with kidney failure, there is usually profuse watery urine production to begin with, turning to very little urine production in the last stages of the disease.

Treatment for kidney failure depends on the cause. There are specific treatments available for infections and toxicity of the kidneys as described under those sections. Unfortunately, there are limited treatments available for kidney failure itself. Intravenous fluids and diuretics, which are drugs to help keep bodily fluids flowing through the kidneys, are just about the only things available. We have no dialysis machines for animals, which is the treatment of choice in people with kidney failure. I have treated many cats and kittens for kidney failure with mixed results. All these cases should be considered very serious.

Antifreeze (Ethylene Glycol) Poisoning

The classic form of antifreeze is a compound called *Ethylene Glycol*. This is a very sweet-smelling liquid that keeps your car radiator from freezing in the winter, but just a few licks of it can cause a fatal acute kidney failure in kittens (and other animals and children). The ethylene glycol precipitates out in the kidneys forming crystals which shut a kidney down. The kittens starts showing symptoms within several hours of ingesting the antifreeze. Symptoms include: vomiting and diarrhea, staggering and incoordination, coma and death. Diagnosis is made by a complete history of the ingestion of the antifreeze, a blood ethylene glycol level, and a urinalysis, which shows many *Oxalate* crystals typical in these case of toxicity. Treatment of early diagnosed cases is intravenous fluids and ethanol (vodka) which help bind and flush out the poison. Many of these kittens die of this poisoning. *Please don't leave out any antifreeze!*

Disease Info Box

Disease	Kidney failure
Common Symptoms	Vomiting, weight loss, oral blisters, abdominal pain, increased thirst and urine output, pale mucus membranes, bloody urine, coma
Diagnosis	X-ray, abdominal ultrasound, blood BUN and Creatinine levels, urinalysis, blood ethylene glycol level
Treatment Options	IV fluids, diuretics, IV ethanol, antibiotics, kidney transplant

Feline Urological Syndrome (FUS)

Feline Urological Syndrome, called *FUS*, is a condition caused by having an excess of certain minerals in the diet or water. The mineral most talked about is magnesium, but others (phosphorous and calcium) can lead to FUS as well. Collectively, we call minerals and salts *dietary ash*.

Kittens with FUS have sand, grit, stones, and crystals in their urinary bladder. Where did these minerals come from? The food, of course! Most commercial cat and kitten diets are very heavy in minerals and salts, because they make the food tasty. The body takes what it needs for strong healthy bones and teeth, muscles, and so forth, and filters out the excess through the kidneys and excretes it with the urine—or, more accurately, leaves it sitting at the bottom of the urinary bladder. These minerals combine to form crystals, which can combine to form gritty stones. These stones, also called *uroliths*, can combine with proteins in the urine to form even larger stones.

The stones scrape the lining of the urinary bladder every time your kitten urinates leading to inflammation, pain, and, ultimately, cystitis.

When your kitten tries to pass these stones, they hurt, causing pain and inflammation. Both male and female kittens can get this disease. In female kittens, the stones pass more readily because their urethra is larger. In male kittens, the *penile urethra* (the tube that carries urine through the penis) is very narrow and these stones get caught there. This urine blockage is called *urethral obstruction*. This is a very serious condition and needs immediate veterinary care. If this obstruction is not relieved within eight hours, there can be irreparable kidney damage leading to kidney failure.

Male kittens who are obstructed strain in their litter box over and over. They may cry or pass a bit of bloody liquid. As soon as they try to urinate, they become frustrated because they cannot pass any urine and their bladder keeps filling. It is very uncomfortable. They usually have abdominal pain, fever, and are very agitated. They will go in and out of their litter box dozens of times hoping that they will be able to urinate.

The diagnosis is very easy for an experienced veterinarian, who can palpate the over-filled urinary bladder. Care must be taken in handling these cats so as not to rupture the bladder.

Treatment usually consists of sedating the male kitten and passing a small plastic catheter into the penis and up into the bladder. The catheter flushes out the obstruction in most cases, allowing the bladder to empty. The cat is kept in the hospital for a couple of days, or until he can urinate on his own, once the catheter is removed.

Your vet will have to take a blood sample to check for kidney damage. Cortisone is sometimes given to relieve the pain and swelling of the urethra, making urinations less painful. Occasionally if the bladder wall was stretched too much when it was overfilled, it can do temporary nerve damage resulting in a paralyzed bladder. This is called an *Atonic Bladder*. There is also medication to help bring back the muscle control so the kitten can urinate voluntarily. Otherwise your vet will have to manually express the bladder when it fills several times daily.

In a small percentage of cases, your veterinarian will not be able to pass the catheter and surgery is the only option to relieve the obstruction. The surgery is called an *urethrostomy* procedure. In this surgery, the male penis is removed and the urethra is opened to allow the stones to pass.

Once the obstruction is relieved, either by a catheter or surgery, your kitten is placed on antibiotics, and a low magnesium diet in hope of preventing another episode. These low ash diets come as canned or dry, and can be found in the grocery store or pet store. Read the ingredients label— the percentage of magnesium should be less than 0.1%. If your veterinarian thinks it wise, there are prescription cat diets and medications that dissolve small bladder stones.

Disease Info Box

Disease	Feline Urological Syndrome (FUS)
Common Symptoms	Continual straining to urinate, crying out in the litter box, bloody urine
Diagnosis	Physical exam, x-ray, kidney blood tests
Treatment Options	Urethral catheter, low ash diets, stone dissolving medication and diets, anti-spasm medications, urinary bladder flush

Chapter 20

Kittens Into Cats

Well, you made it! Congratulations. It was a long journey through your kitten's health, but by now you are an expert in practical kitten care. I'm sure it was worth the effort. As your precious little bundle of fluff and love turns into a mature adult cat, her needs will be different. Let me go through a few points.

Maintaining Good Health

All those chapters in part one of this book are still useful now. All those good tips and healthy ideas regarding eye, ear and coat care still apply. Go back

This is how beautiful and healthy your kitten can be with proper care. *Tammy Thomas, Pet Pics of Rags R Us Libby.*

and refresh your memory. Adult cats need regular health maintenance. In fact, as your kitten gets older, it will become even more important.

Nutrition is also important. Adult cats have different nutritional needs than kittens, but the principles are the same—proper nutrition with good eating habits.

Kittens aren't the only cats who need vaccinations and worming. Adult cats get annual boosters of all the diseases enumerated in chapter two. Although some of the diseases were presented as kittenhood diseases, many adult cats can get them just the same.

How about that first aid and household chapter? Cats need first aid, too. And don't think adult cats don't still try to get into household dangers. Believe me, they still try. So this information is still very pertinent for your now adult cat.

You probably noticed as you were reading the pediatrics chapters that a lot of the diseases and conditions are also found in adult cats. So don't file this book away and let it collect dust. You will find yourself pulling it off the shelf regularly. Probably every time you go see your veterinarian.

Kittens Grow into Cats

Your kitten is approaching adulthood. He's growing bigger and stronger. He may be more sharp, alert and agile. His needs change, but the basics of kitten care still apply. Maybe you noticed he isn't as affectionate as he was as a kitten. All these things are normal. As your kitten grows, you will grow with him. Learn what his new needs and wants are—maybe more play time, or more regular grooming. The worst thing you can do is grow apart and lose the bond you had when he was little. This can happen if you allow him to become an outdoor cat, or if other things in your life distract your attentions.

Keeping Your Vet Involved

Most new kitten owners find themselves at their veterinarian's office for all the routine kitten visits. Remember all the vaccinations, well visits, worming, and frantic calls about things you had no clue about? Now things have slowed down a little. Maybe you aren't visiting the clinic as often, but that doesn't mean you shouldn't keep your vet involved in your cat's health. Ask him or her about your cat's new needs and expectations. Never feel inhibited about calling your vet for advice. As your cat ages there will be new problems and concerns. My point is simple: Just because your kitten is grown up doesn't mean your vet's job is over. On the contrary—it has just begun.

Appendix I

Feline Registries

There are six purebred cat registries in the United States. The CFA is the largest, but you can contact any of them for information about the breeds in their registry, rules and regulations, cat shows, or to help you find a pedigreed cat.

American Association of Cat Enthusiasts
P.O. Box 213
Pine Brook, NJ 07058

American Cat Association
8101 Katherine Avenue
Panorama City, CA 91402

American Cat Fanciers' Association (ACFA)
P.O. Box 203
Pt. Lookout, MO 65726

Cat Fanciers' Association (CFA)
P.O. Box 1005
Manasquan, NJ 08736-0805

Cat Fanciers' Federation
9509 Montgomery Road
Cincinnati, OH 45242

The International Cat Association (TICA)
P.O. Box 2684
Harlingen, TX 78551

GENERAL INDEX

Printed in the USA
CPSIA information can be obtained
at www.ICGtesting.com
JSHW012015140824
68134JS00025B/2438

9 780876 057636